THE INSPIRED HOUSEPLANT

TRANSFORM YOUR HOME WITH INDOOR PLANTS

from Kokedama to Terrariums
and Water Gardens to Edibles

JEN STEARNS

 SASQUATCH BOOKS
SEATTLE

Printed in China

Published by Sasquatch Books

23 22 21 20 19   9 8 7 6 5 4 3 2 1

Editor: Hannah Elnan
Design: Tony Ong
Photography: Unless otherwise noted, interior photography
    provided by © Sara Mark Photography
Copyeditor: Kirsten Colton

Library of Congress Cataloging-in-Publication Data
    Names: Stearns, Jen, author.
    Title: The inspired houseplant : transform your home with indoor plants from
        kokedama to terrariums and water gardens to edibles / Jen Stearns.
    Description: Seattle, WA : Sasquatch Books, [2019]
    Identifiers: LCCN 2018014482 | ISBN 9781632171771 (hardback)
    Subjects: LCSH: House plants.
    Classification: LCC SB419 .S698 2019 | DDC 635.9/65--dc23
    LC record available at https://lccn.loc.gov/2018014482

ISBN: 978-1-63217-177-1

Sasquatch Books
1904 Third Avenue, Suite 710
Seattle, WA 98101
(206) 467-4300
SasquatchBooks.com

GIRL FRIDAY
PRODUCTIONS®

CONTENTS

Introduction   ix

I. PLANT BASICS

Prepare Your Planting Kit   5   Prune Your Way to Happiness   21

Master the Art of Potting   9   Rethink Feeding Your Plants   29

Conquer Your Watering Fears   15

II. PLANT GUIDE

Environmental Zones   36   **Tropical Plants**   **55**

Desert Plants   **39**   Calathea (Marantaceae)   55

Air Plant (Bromeliaceae)   39   Cast-Iron Plant (Asparagaceae) 56

Cactus (Cactaceae)   40   Citrus (Rutaceae)   59

Echeveria (Crassulaceae)   43   Dieffenbachia (Araceae)   60

Palm (Arecaceae)   44   Dracaena (Asparagaceae)   63

Snake Plant (Asparagaceae)   47   Ficus (Moraceae)   64

Temperate Plants   **49**   Nerve Plant (Acanthaceae)   67

Fern (Polypodiaceae)   49   Pothos (Araceae)   68

Peace Lily (Araceae)   50   **Aquatic Plants**   **71**

Sempervivum (Crassulaceae)   53   Lucky Bamboo (Asparagaceae)   71

                                          Marimo (Cladophoraceae)   72

III. PLANT PROJECTS

Terrariums and Bowl Gardens 79

    Tropical Terrarium 81

    Succulent Bowl 87

    Hanging Air Plant Globe 93

Water Gardens 97

    Marimo Habitat 99

    Underwater Landscape 103

    Floating Stems 109

Hanging and Vertical Gardens 113

    Kokedama 115

    Reflected Pyramid Himmeli 121

    Vertical Vines 129

    Mounted Staghorn Fern 133

The Kitchen Garden 137

    Veggie Reincarnation 139

    Living Herb Frame 149

IV. PLANT STYLE

Desert Boho 159

Eclectic 163

Midcentury 167

Minimal 171

Rustic 175

Urban Oasis 179

Acknowledgments 183
Resources 185
Index 189
Photo Credits 192

INTRODUCTION

Most of us have memories from childhood of indoor plants that seemed somehow part of the family. Maybe it was a classic Boston fern hanging from the ceiling, or a potted cactus or bamboo, or a ficus in the corner. What many people don't have to go along with those memories, however, is the knowledge of or confidence in how to take care of indoor plants of their own. I used to teach people how to grow food in an urban setting. Along the way, I realized how many folks of all ages weren't ready for that because they had an outright fear of plants. "Can't grow a thing," they told me. "I can kill a plant just by looking at it." And I knew the type because while my mother had a beautiful garden outside our Pacific Northwest home (with a little plot always set aside for me), she had a brown thumb indoors! Some people consider owning a houseplant to being akin to owning a dog in terms of responsibility. I must disagree there. While it's true that like dogs, certain breeds of plants are better suited to certain owners, a plant requires far less care and less responsibility, and it's much easier to learn how to do it right.

After I realized it was fear holding so many people back, I made it my mission to give people the skills and the confidence to play with indoor plants and to use greenery to create a sense of home in their space. Think about what a space without plants feels like: clinical, sterile. Now add plants. Homey, right? Warm, designed, cared for. There's real science behind all those fuzzy feelings; studies show that office production goes up when there are plants in the office and that dopamine levels rise for people with plants in the home, especially if they help handle them and care for them. An often-cited study by the National Aeronautics and Space Administration (NASA) also found that certain indoor plants do a fantastic job of filtering our interior air of chemicals. While NASA studied a specific list of cultivars, all indoor plants work to filter the air and add oxygen in varying amounts, so the more plants the better! What I love about plants is that the beauty, joy, and health that plants bring to us indoors are accessible to everyone. Black thumb or no, there is truly a plant for you, and in this book you'll find all the information to demystify plant ownership, including potting, watering, pruning, and feeding, as well as a guide to some of the most common houseplants organized by their environmental needs so you can easily pick the plants that both appeal to your aesthetics and suit your home environment and caretaking style.

NATURE'S AIR FILTER

In the late 1980s, NASA commissioned a joint study to determine how well certain plants work to clean inside air and remove dangerous and cancer-causing toxins such as benzene, formaldehyde, and trichloroethylene from the interior of buildings. This was in response to the rise of "sick building syndrome," with symptoms not attributable to any specific disease, which the World Health Organization postulated was affecting a growing number of inhabitants of new construction. The results are perhaps not surprising: plants do a remarkable job of helping to clean our air and keep us healthy. The following are all plants listed in Part II: Plant Guide (page 32) that get a thumb's-up from NASA—though remember, all indoor plants contribute to a healthy environment:

- Dracaena (page 63)
- Palm (page 44)
- Snake plant (page 47)
- Peace lily (page 50)
- Pothos (page 68)

But plants don't just clean our air and generate a sense of Zen. They're also design powerhouses, able to play into completely different looks and design aesthetics and act as statement pieces or subtle decor. Inside this book you'll find everything you need to feel confident in bringing plants in all their glory into your space. Both those who live in tiny apartments and those with a host of spacious rooms to fill will find just the right look to highlight a plant as well as brighten a corner or bring drama to a tabletop. Because while many of us hold cherished memories of Grandma's plants, we don't necessarily want to replicate her aesthetic. Whether you're partial to an untamed lush look or want a touch of modern minimalism, indoor plants are incredibly versatile. The projects in this book are meant to highlight what makes each type of plant special, whether it's a striking pattern on the foliage or a cool texture to the leaf, and let you customize your designs. Don't fret if you're not crafty; some projects are more advanced while others involve nothing more than tying a knot. Both beginning and more experienced indoor gardeners should begin by reading Part I: Plant Basics (page xii) and Part II: Plant Guide (page 32), both primers of sorts to give you a good base of knowledge before choosing your first project from Part III: Plant Projects (page 74). After you've mastered the basics, Part IV: Plant Style (page 154) gives you a range of looks to inspire you and get you started on creating your own designs. Your indoor gardens can get as creative as you dare. Ready? Let's dive in and turn your space into a gorgeous garden paradise.

I. PLANT
BASICS

Filled with tips and tricks for even experienced gardeners, this chapter is a must-read for beginners and those who think they have black thumbs. Because there is no magic to good plant care, just basic science and simple rules.

Prepare Your Planting Kit   5

Master the Art of Potting   9

Conquer Your Watering Fears   15

Prune Your Way to Happiness   21

Rethink Feeding Your Plants   29

PREPARE YOUR PLANTING KIT

If you wanted to bake a cake, you'd need both quality ingredients and the right size bowl, mixer, and pan. Successful indoor gardening is no different. While you can make it work with minimal and inexpensive tools, having the right ones on hand will make your work a breeze.

TOOLS OF THE TRADE

In truth, you probably already have all the tools you need to do basic indoor gardening, but, like with most things, there are also certain specialty items to aid in your (and your plant's!) success.

Must-Haves

HANDS: Your hands are the most important tools you have! Don't be afraid to get in there and get dirty—that's half the fun of planting and potting. If you want to keep soil from getting under your nails, run your nails over a bar of soap, like you're scratching it, to fill in the space underneath. After planting, wash your hands and the dirt will come right out.

GLOVES: I almost never use garden gloves when working indoors, though they are necessary for handling cacti. However, most people like to keep their hands neat and clean and spare the manicure. Buy a snug pair that offers good dexterity and grip, since you'll be working with smaller objects.

SNIPS: The one piece of "industry" equipment I must insist on are good-quality snips (or clippers)—they look like a pair of specialty scissors. They are the only tool you should use for trimming roots and pruning. Their edges are razor sharp, which spares the plant by making clean, surgical cuts. A good pair is not that expensive. Make sure to maintain them by wiping them down after use and keeping them dry.

WATERING CAN AND MISTER: You can buy very inexpensive watering cans and spray bottles for a few dollars, or spend some

money to buy ones that are a pleasure to use and that are so pretty you want to keep them out. Of course, you can also use many types of household containers you already have for watering, even a margarita pitcher!

Nice-to-Haves

While not essential, these items are especially useful for creating more intricate projects or working with smaller indoor plants.

SCOOP OR A TROWEL: Useful for adding dirt or porous substrate to pots and digging planting holes. Measuring cups work well in a pinch too; just wash them after use.

CHOPSTICKS: Great for poking holes in soil to make space for roots, (carefully) aerating the soil in your pots, or placing items in delicate pots.

TWEEZERS: Useful for doing delicate work in terrariums or small bowls.

ORGANIZATION: Since most indoor gardeners don't have a reserved space for creating projects, where a potting shed might function outdoors, keeping tools and supplies both tidy and at the ready allows you to create on a moment's notice—without creating a mess.

PLASTIC TOTE AND CONTAINERS: While outdoor gardeners can throw all their tools in a shed, apartment dwellers or those without storage don't have the luxury. A stacking plastic tote works well for holding all your tools and pots. For those short on space, an under-the-bed plastic storage container works as well. Plastic containers meant to hold large amounts of cereal or grains are nice for storing soil, compost, or fertilizer.

KRAFT PAPER: Sturdy, hard to tear, and compostable, kraft paper is available in craft and hardware stores and makes a great surface for planting. Plasticized tablecloths, like those meant for picnics or outdoor tables, also work quite well.

COTTON TWINE OR JUTE: Gardening twine or jute can be used to tie a plant to a support, repair a kokedama or mounted fern, extend training lines for vines, or even tie bundles of herbs together for drying.

APRON: One with pockets can hold your tools while you're working and keep your clothes clean.

ARE HOUSEPLANTS SAFE FOR KIDS AND PETS?

The short answer is: it varies. Widely. While some plants are considered so safe they are commonly used in food displays (echeveria), and others are notorious for causing bad reactions in animals (aloe), even "safe" plants can cause tummy aches in kids and pets while others could cause even more severe reactions, including death. If you have kids or pets, consult your doctor or your vet and tell them about the plants you have in the house. They will be able to give you more detailed information on the possible dangers of each and the threshold for toxicity. Use common sense and move plants to where children and pets can't reach them, especially with small children or young animals who like to chew on everything! See Resources (page 185) for some online sources that offer details to supplement the information your child's or your pet's health provider gives you.

MASTER THE ART OF POTTING

Successful repotting of indoor plants is easy, with just a few basic rules to keep in mind that I've outlined below. In general, it's a good idea to repot any plant you bring home within about two months' time as plants don't enjoy living in plastic nursery pots for long periods. In addition, don't forget about repotting your existing cultivars to keep them looking and feeling their best. Plants in a 2-gallon pot or smaller should be repotted once a year. Plants in larger pots can go between 2 and 3 years before repotting.

CHOOSE THE RIGHT POT

- If you want a plant to get bigger, give it more space. Going up by 2 inches in diameter when repotting is a common rule of thumb, but you can give your plant more room if you really want to encourage growth. This is because the root system largely mirrors the canopy above, and giving the root ball more space encourages the plant to do the same topside.
- If you want a plant to stay the same size, you can repot in the same-size pot so long as you trim the roots prior to repotting. See Below the Soil (page 24) for instructions on how to trim the roots correctly.
- You must water more carefully if you plant in a cachepot, a type of pot without drainage holes. Pots with drainage holes and watertight trays beneath give you more leeway for making overwatering mistakes. See Conquer Your Watering Fears (page 15) for more information.

ADD A DRAINAGE LAYER

- Before potting a plant in any pot, whether it has drainage holes or not, put a drainage layer down in the form of bark, pebbles, chunks of clean cement, or even shards of broken pottery in the bottom of the pot. Not only does this keep soil from running out the drainage holes (if present), but it prevents the roots from sitting in water.
- Your drainage layer should be between 1 and 3 inches deep depending on the size of the pot, with larger-diameter pots sporting the deeper layers.

OUT WITH THE OLD

- Repotting nearly always requires really getting into the root mass with your fingers, loosening and separating the individual roots and shaking off as much of the old soil as possible. Doing this step ensures the roots get out of their binding pattern and grow more effectively. Removing the old soil means they can better access the nutrients in their fresh, new soil. When you're in the process of removing the old soil, don't be concerned if you hear slight tearing sounds coming from the roots. Most plants can lose up to two-thirds of their root mass and come out okay, so slight damage at this point isn't detrimental.
- A few fussy cultivars (these include begonias, ficus, and cacti) don't like having their roots touched. When repotting these plants, disturb them as little as possible during the transfer.

BEST POTTING SOILS FOR DIFFERENT PLANT TYPES

Part II: Plant Guide (page 32) is divided into different types of growing environments. Below, you'll find the right type of potting soil for each of those plant types. If you can't be bothered to make your own potting-soil mixes, most plants will do just fine with organic all-purpose potting soil from the store; I recommend Black Gold brand. The exception is desert plants. They need a special fast-draining substrate to thrive.

Plants from Desert Zones

Plants that you water infrequently, such as most succulents, don't want to be planted in plain dirt. They prefer a mix made up of mostly nonorganic matter like different types of rock and bark pieces that allow water to drain quickly and the roots to have access to air. Create your own desert mix using standard potting soil and either washed pea gravel or sand in a 1:1 ratio, or make it easier on yourself and buy a ready-made cactus or succulent potting mix. There are many different brands out there; I like the cactus mix by Black Gold.

Plants from Temperate Zones

These species love loamy soils rich in organic matter, which translates into a general potting soil with some compost and small pieces of substrate for drainage mixed in. Use a 2:1 ratio of potting soil to compost, with a handful of small rocks or pebbles.

Plants from Tropical Zones

A good general potting soil with no compost added is best for tropical plants, as compost is too heavy for these plants.

I just potted my plant and now the lower leaves are turning yellow and dropping. What did I do wrong?

Your plant is probably suffering from transplant shock, the name for the reaction a plant has to your handling and to its new environment. Certain plant species are more susceptible, but to minimize transplant shock in most species, treat the roots with care, make sure to water thoroughly at the time of replanting with a bacterial inoculant solution, and place in bright light for at least a few days following replanting. Most plants recover within about a week. Leaves that are damaged or discolored during this process won't recover (you can trim them off), but so long as no new leaves turn brown or yellow, you're in the clear.

HOW TO POT A PLANT

1   Place a nonporous drainage layer in the bottom of the pot.

2   Add a thin layer of potting soil, filling in the holes and just covering the drainage layer.

3   Take the plant out of the old pot, turning the pot on its side and patting the bottom gently to loosen the plant if necessary. Rake your fingers through the roots gently and shake off any loose soil. (For fussy plants like begonias, ficus, or cacti, don't rake or shake.)

4   If you are not going up a pot size, use snips to trim the roots. Big, thick roots usually indicate the plant has more root ball than it needs.

5   Holding the plant with one hand, fan out the roots in the bottom of the pot. Scoop soil around and on top of the roots, leaving at least ½ inch at the top of the pot to catch water overflow.

6   Pat the soil down lightly to firm it. Water immediately with bacterial inoculant (see Create Healthy Soil, page 30).

How can I tell if a plant needs to be repotted?
A plant that needs a refresh will show symptoms of root binding and nutrient deficiency. If you haven't changed the watering schedule or the placement of the plant, and suddenly the lower leaves begin to yellow or drop, or the plant just looks droopy, even after watering and feeding, try repotting with fresh soil in a larger pot.

GENERAL WATERING GUIDELINES

LEAFY PLANTS

TEMPERATE

BUTTON FERN
- Likes moisture
- Water daily

TROPICAL

PEACE LILY
- Water weekly

RIGID PLANTS

DESERT

AIR PLANT
- Needs periodic soaking or misting (see page 39)

DESERT

CACTUS
- Water every 3–6 weeks

CONQUER YOUR WATERING FEARS

Fear of under- or overwatering plants is real, and most beginning gardeners (even pros!) want that one golden rule that they can apply to watering their plants to make sure they do it right. Unfortunately, that one golden rule doesn't exist, because there are so many variables that can affect how thirsty plants become as well as how often. Drafts, relative humidity, air-conditioning, heating, pots that are more or less porous, the size of the container . . . all of these factors affect watering. That said, below are some general tips that you can apply to plants within your home. As you become more comfortable with your plants and different types of containers and projects, the needs of the plant will become more apparent to you.

I have heard that cacti don't need water. Is that true?
One of the most common misconceptions about plants that need infrequent watering (cacti, air plants, snake plants) is that they don't need water at all. Especially indoors, all plants need some water and nutrients to live; some just need less than others. See Part II: Plant Guide (page 32) for detailed information on different plant types. Cacti, for example, want fast-draining soil and should be watered every 3 to 6 weeks or so, depending on the humidity of your home.

GENERAL WATERING GUIDELINES

- Leafy plants tend to want to stay moister, while plants with more rigid structures, including cacti, snake plants, or plants with woody stems, need less water. Use this info to help you choose the best plant for you. Do you love to water? Choose faster-growing and leafier plants. A bit neglectful? Choose plants with rigid or thicker leaves and stems.
- No potted plant likes to sit in water. If water goes out into the drainage tray under the pot and stays for more than a day, dump it out. When repotting, make sure to include a drainage layer in the bottom of the pot.

- Smaller pots or containers need to be watered more often in general. That said, many people tend to overwater bigger pots, thinking they need to saturate every inch of soil. A very general rule is to use water equal to about one-third the volume of the pot, so long as the pot contains a drainage hole.
- When watering a plant in a cachepot (no drainage hole), cut the water volume in half and double the frequency of watering. Adding a layer of rock or gravel to the bottom of the pot before planting will give you a little more leeway with overwatering. You'll get a feel for the plant's needs as you go along.
- A regular schedule may help beginning gardeners who have trouble telling by look or feel if it's time to water. Pick a day (or several, depending on the needs of your plants) and make it a routine. Don't get stuck in your regular habit, however. When you bring a new plant into your home, reassess, and make sure the newcomer will work with the routine. If not, change it up.
- There is a lot of information on the internet that says you should use only filtered or bottled water on indoor plants. I think that if you are comfortable drinking your tap water, you can feed it to plants. If you know your water is super chlorinated, you can let the chlorine dissipate by leaving the water out for a couple of days before watering.

Am I overwatering my plant?
An easy way to tell if you're overwatering your plant is if there's water pouring into the saucer underneath your pot. No plant likes sitting in excess water; some hate it so much they'll commit suicide. If you notice lots of extra water in your saucer, simply pour it off after a day and water a bit less the next time. As a rule, plants with leafy foliage (such as ferns) like more water and more humid environments, while plants with firmer structures and leaves (such as snake plants) need less water overall.

HOW TO WATER YOUR PLANTS

Twice a week, look over the plants in your home and evaluate them for watering. This is what you look for:

Signs of Overwatering

- musty smell
- soil that never dries out
- small insects (like flies or gnats) on the surface of the soil
- bottom leaves turning yellow
- bottom leaves turning brown
- mushy leaves or mushy spots

Signs of Underwatering

- drooping
- shriveling
- leaf tips or edges that are crispy and brown
- leaves in middle or near the top that are yellowing

As a caveat, a plant that needs to be repotted because it is root-bound or has nutrient-poor soil could exhibit the same signs as underwatering. If you haven't changed your watering schedule and your plant exhibits these signs, either repot with organic all-purpose potting soil and water with bacterial inoculant, or just break up the first inch or so of soil with your fingers or a fork and mix in a little fresh potting soil to tide the plant over until you can (see Master the Art of Potting, page 9).

WATERING TERRARIUMS AND OTHER CLOSED CONTAINERS

Because terrariums retain moisture so effectively, different watering rules apply than for regular potted plants or open container gardens. Follow these tips for best results:

- A spray bottle allows you to apply the moisture evenly and lightly and keep the soil moist but not wet.
- If you see any pooling in the bottom of your terrarium, you need to stop and water less.
- To water terrariums without removing the lid, pour water equivalent to one-quarter of the volume of the tray into the gravel. If water remains in the gravel and pools, you have watered too much. Remove the lid to allow some of the moisture to dissipate before replacing it, and water less the next time.
- When checking the water level of your terrarium, light condensation is okay, but it shouldn't look heavy like a steam shower. In cases of excess condensation, simply leave the lid off for a day, then replace.

GET SOME HELP FROM TECH

For potted plants, there are excellent tools to help the plant take up as much water as it needs—and not a drop more. My favorite is the Blumat, a terra-cotta spike made in Austria that siphons water via plastic tubing from a vessel you keep topped off. This allows the plant to take only as much water as it needs and is especially useful for long absences or vacations. I find that similar devices that depend on gravity rather than osmosis to water the plant do not work very well.

Water-sensing devices, from strips to color-changing objects to electronic sensors like the Thirsty Light, are popular with some people to help them know the proper time to water. However, these devices work only for plants that can tolerate drying out fully between drinks, because it is the complete absence of moisture that triggers the indication to water.

How do you water hanging plants?
The best way to water all types of hanging plants is to first take them down. Not only will this spare your furniture or your floors, but some hanging projects, like kokedama (page 115), need to be soaked. To keep glass vessels clear and sparkling, remove air plants from hanging orbs before misting or soaking. Place other plants in a tub or shower before watering and allow them to drain completely before rehanging.

LET THERE BE LIGHT

The most popular houseplants tend to be tolerant of different lighting conditions. While they may not go crazy in lighting that is nonideal, most won't die either. That said, taking care to select plants for the lighting conditions you have will yield better results and happier plants. Remember: *all* plants need some light to grow. A few hardy types, including lucky bamboo and the cast-iron plant, can live on fluorescent light alone, making them popular choices for office buildings and windowless spaces. All others need natural light from windows to give them what they need. Alternatively, grow lights can be placed in fixtures or lamps and set on timers (see Resources, page 185) to make up for a lack of natural lighting. Below are common lighting terms demystified to help guide your choices:

LOW LIGHT: Plants should be placed within a few feet of an east- or north-facing window, or across the room from or with an obstructed view of a south- or west-facing window. Peace lily, philodendron, and calathea are common low-light plants.

MODERATE LIGHT: Plant should be placed next to an east- or north-facing window and receive at least a few hours of direct light each day. Most houseplants that tolerate low light *love* moderate light. Arrowhead plants, purple passion plants, and prayer plants all enjoy moderate light.

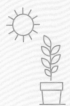

BRIGHT LIGHT: Plants that want bright light need to inhabit an area that gets direct exposure for 6-plus hours a day and/or be placed in front of a south- or west-facing window. Citrus, succulents like echeveria, and cacti all thrive in bright light.

DIFFUSED LIGHT: This means the sunlight is passing through some filter before hitting the plant. Examples include frosted glass, a sheer curtain, or a tree that obscures the window. Plants that need diffused light will burn in direct sun.

DIRECT LIGHT: Sunlight that hits a plant through a window unimpeded by tree leaves, curtains, or any other filters is called direct light. Plants that need direct light crave both the light and the heat that direct light brings.

PRUNE YOUR WAY
TO HAPPINESS

Outdoor gardeners spend a good bit of time pruning, but for indoor gardeners, it's almost always an aesthetic choice whether to prune, rather than a necessity for good care. For tropical plants, a category that includes some of the most popular houseplants, pruning can be used to encourage a desired growth habit but isn't necessary. Cacti don't want to be pruned at all. If you find yourself wanting to maintain or create a desired shape for types of indoor plants other than cacti, make sure you don't prune off more than a third of the plant at any time and follow the rules below for healthy pruning according to plant shape.

ABOVE THE SOIL

There are four basic shapes of indoor plants that you might need to prune, each of them needing a specific method to achieve the best results.

Treelike Form

This form is exhibited by any plant that has branches, such as citrus. Anywhere one branch intersects with another branch is called a node. This is a hormone site for the plant, and for plants, just like for people, hormones are necessary for growth. When pruning a branching plant, you will always want to use your snips to cut right above a node at a 45-degree angle. This encourages a bushier growth habit rather than allowing the plant to become tall and lean, what we in the plant world call *leggy*. When you prune above a node, two or more branches (even up to four) will emerge from the node.

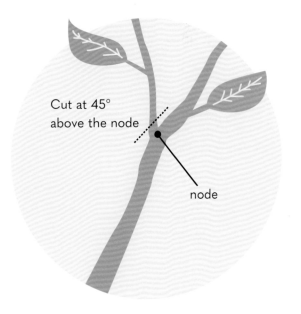

Cut at 45°
above the node

node

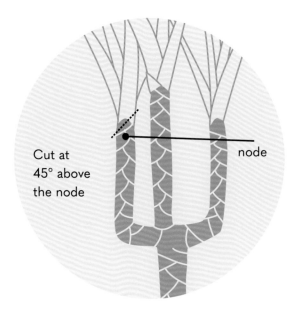

Cut at
45° above
the node   node

Stalk Oriented

Plants that are more stalk oriented,
like the dracaena, require a different
approach. These plants grow by
sending out a stalk, or cluster of
leaves, off a central stem. Once a new
stalk has emerged, you don't want to
top it or cut across the stalk. Once
the stalk is more mature and there is
visible stem underneath, you can find
a node and, using your snips, prune
above the node at a 45-degree angle.
Either let the cut air dry or apply wax
to help seal the wound.

Circular Pattern

Plants like palms, succulents, and air
plants have layers of foliage growing
in a circular pattern. For these types
of plants, it is natural that lower
branches might turn brown. If they do,
you should be able to peel them off
with a gentle tug. Succulents are the
most common plants with this growth
pattern that you might want to prune.
You might notice that instead of being
the cute little rosettes you started off
with, they have shot up and gotten
too leggy for your liking. Take your
snips and cut anywhere along the stem
below the rosette.

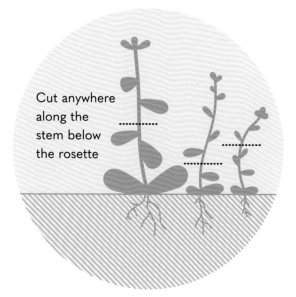

Cut anywhere
along the
stem below
the rosette

CREATING CUTTINGS

The added benefit of pruning succulents is that you can now root that pruned rosette and create a new plant. After pruning, allow the cut rosette to dry at room temperature so that the stem can callous. You are looking for the plant to form a dry "scab" over the cut portion of stem—anywhere from 2 days to a week should do it. This step is essential if you want your succulent to root rather than rot. Once it's ready, pop it into moist soil and it should root quickly. Use the same process to trim off "chicks" from a hen and chicks succulent (see Sempervivum, page 53) or even from different types of plants. Air plants, for example, reproduce by growing "pups" that can be trimmed off in the same way.

Ground Covers

These plants, such as spike moss (*Selaginella* species), are composed of tons of tiny little branches, each with its own root system. Control the spread of this type of plant by giving it a haircut with your snips, much like you would trim a hedge, just snipping off the foliage until it reaches the length you want.

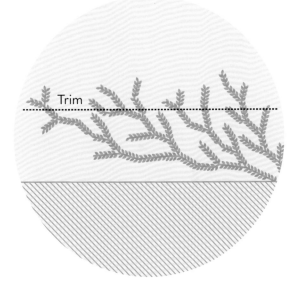

BELOW THE SOIL

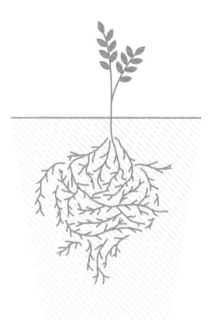

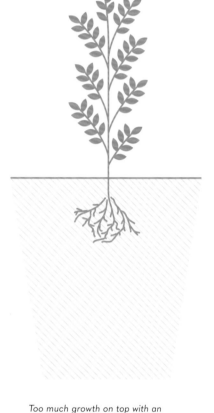

Too large of a root ball (especially water roots) overloads the plant; it's like a fire hose shooting water up to stems and leaves that can't use everything they're getting.

Too much growth on top with an insufficient root system means the plant lacks the equipment necessary to take in what it needs to thrive.

While many people think of pruning plants aboveground, what they don't realize is that the root systems of plants are meant to reflect and mirror the branching systems above. Plants with shallow root systems and heavy branches are out of sync; so too are plants with spare stems and leaves but very robust root systems. Pruning the roots equalizes the two, reducing transplant shock and trauma and creating a more balanced system for the plant.

Every plant with roots has two different kinds: water roots and nutrient roots. If you look at a root system closely, you can easily tell the difference, as water roots are thicker channels than nutrient roots. Think of a dandelion: it has one giant water root (the one you so desperately want to pull from your lawn) and many smaller nutrient roots that look like threads or tiny filaments. The more water roots a plant has, the faster and bigger it can grow. Nutrient roots channel to the plant the trace minerals and elements from the soil that it needs.

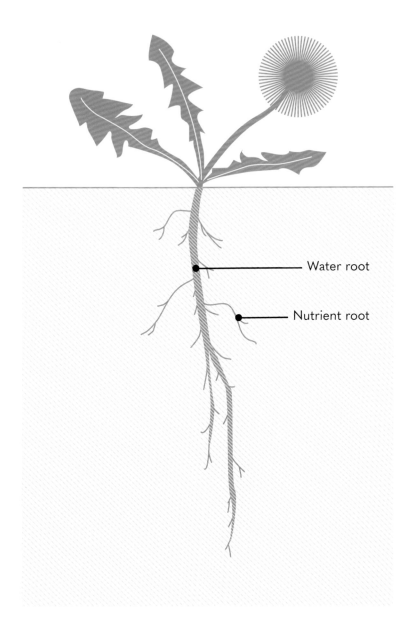

Reasons for Root Trimming

Though many beginning gardeners are terrified of the idea of cutting off any of a plant's root system, there are certain cases when this is exactly what the plant requires.

DWARFING: If you want to dwarf the size of your plant, you want to reduce the number of water roots it has. Just as with pruning above the soil, to do this, take your snips and cut right below two intersecting roots. Just as with branches, intersections in root systems signal the existence of a node. To get the hang of pruning root systems, you may want to practice on plants that don't mind so much. I find the jade plant, for example, especially forgiving; you wouldn't want to make a ficus or cactus your first attempt, as they require much more care.

ROOT-BOUND: When you buy a new plant and take it out of its pot, you might find your plant is root-bound, a condition where the roots are too substantial for their enclosed space and have kept searching for escape, circling around and around the pot until they effectively strangle the plant. While replanting into a larger pot helps, for the plant to thrive, you also need to trim back the bound roots so that they are in harmony with the size of the plant. Using your fingers, pull apart the roots as best you can, using some force if necessary to free the roots from their entanglement. Locate a few of the largest water roots and clip them back so that the plant will concentrate on getting healthy again and catch up on top.

PLANT HARMONY: Root trimming also helps plants get along better with their friends, especially when they are chummy in a small environment like an aquarium or a bowl. One of the reasons the spider plant (*Chlorophytum comosum*), one of the most common houseplants, is so prolific is that it has a very aggressive root system. This allows it to produce so many offspring that the spider plant is like the bunny of the plant world. If you trim back the plant's roots, it will coexist more peacefully with other plants in a communal environment.

RETHINK FEEDING YOUR PLANTS

You can grow lush, healthy houseplants without dousing them in commercial fertilizer. In fact, doing so is not good for your household, your plant, or the world, and simply makes you and your plants dependent on chemicals. Create a healthy environment instead and watch them flourish!

FERTILIZER IS A GATEWAY DRUG

When and how and how much fertilizer to give plants are some of the most common questions new gardeners have. The good news is that you don't have to memorize ratios of different elements or buy specialized food for each of your plants. There are companies that certainly want you to think that you do, but keep in mind that a lot of that is good marketing and a targeted move from corporations to get you and your plants hooked on their product.

If that sounds extreme, consider this. In nature, plants take in the nutrients they need from the soil, working in symbiosis with the bacteria and fungi in the dirt that receive chemical signals from the plant and get it what it needs.

RULES OF THUMB

To recreate that natural process, it's up to you to keep up an active biota in the very small region that is your potted plant's soil. How often you treat the soil to accomplish that is affected by the size of your container, the relative humidity of the environment, and whether the plant is putting energy toward flowers or fruit.

- Larger containers and moister environments can self-regulate longer without intervention from you.
- For most houseplants, healthy soil negates the need for any other additives.
- Plants that flower or fruit will need more energy to accomplish their goals. They also require more phosphorus than other plants.
- Leafy plants generally require more nitrogen than other plants.

CREATE HEALTHY SOIL

Rather than using commercial fertilizer, every month or two I use a bacterial inoculant on nearly all my plants (see Resources, page 185). While the term sounds scientific, this is basically the same as a compost "tea" used by outdoor gardeners—the fermented liquid made from the waste of worms and other organic matter—but put into granular form that you mix with water and then use to water your plants like usual. The granules are made from a bloom of the bacteria that exist in a complete ecosystem. These bacteria read signals from the organism and react, giving the plant what it needs through a subterranean superhighway.

Dehydrated compost-tea granules reactivate with water nicely. While not quite as good as the real thing, they are organic, safe for kids and pets, won't burn plants, and can be used on any kind of soil. As you use them regularly, you can even begin to undo the damage that chemical additives have done to soil in the past. If you notice a white bloom on top of the soil after using the bacterial inoculant, that's a sign that chemicals existing in the soil have killed the bacteria. Keep at it, and the soil will slowly recover, allowing the bacteria to do its work.

For plants that need it, it is better to buy fertilizer from small organic nurseries than from chain stores, where I've found that additives labeled "organic" are not actually so. Natural amendments are good for adding more nitrogen to the soil, something leafy plants want, or more phosphorus, important for fruiting or flowering cultivars. Apply natural amendments to these types of plants both right before and during their growing season, or when you begin to see more vigorous growth, flowers, or fruit. Natural additives include:

- Worm castings (phosphorus)
- Bat guano (phosphorus)
- Cotton or alfalfa seed meal (nitrogen)
- Fish emulsion (nitrogen, phosphorus, potassium)

PLANTS WITH SPECIAL NEEDS

- Air plants need a specialized foliar fertilizer. *Foliar* means it is sprayed onto the leaves of the plant rather than applied at the roots, which . . . air plants don't have! You can find organic formulas with the numbers "17–8–22" in garden stores and online. The numbers indicate the ratio of nitrogen, phosphorus, and potassium that's in the fertilizer blend. You don't necessarily need to know what those numbers mean, just to look for them. Once a month, after regular misting or soaking, mist thoroughly with the fertilizer. Doing so after watering means the stomata will be open and can better receive the nutrients.
- When planting citrus such as lime, lemon, or orange trees, you need to use richer soil at the outset. Substitute compost or bat guano for up to one-quarter of the potting soil, as the added organic material helps the tree put energy into flowering and fruiting.
- Aquatic plants need the type of slow-release food found in the form of organic pellets or tablets buried in the substrate.
- Single plants in hydroculture (those sitting in water) need organic liquid fertilizer that dissolves into the water. Use liquid fertilizer when it would be unsightly to use pellets or tablets (see Floating Stems, page 109).

SIGNS YOU NEED TO FEED YOUR PLANT

- Lower leaves (those closest to the dirt) begin to yellow or drop, and light and water are appropriate.
- Plants are drooping or wilting, and light and water are appropriate.

II. PLANT GUIDE

Because the main challenge for most indoor gardeners lies with giving their plants appropriate care—knowing how much light they need, for example, or how often to water—the following guide to some of the most popular and intriguing houseplants groups together specimens with similar care and feeding requirements. This way, as you get to know these plants and others like them, you will begin to recognize and anticipate their basic needs.

Environmental Zones 36

Desert Plants **39**

Air Plant (Bromeliaceae) 39

Cactus (Cactaceae) 40

Echeveria (Crassulaceae) 43

Palm (Arecaceae) 44

Snake Plant (Asparagaceae) 47

Temperate Plants **49**

Fern (Polypodiaceae) 49

Peace Lily (Araceae) 50

Sempervivum (Crassulaceae) 53

Tropical Plants **55**

Calathea (Marantaceae) 55

Cast-Iron Plant (Asparagaceae) 56

Citrus (Rutaceae) 59

Dieffenbachia (Araceae) 60

Dracaena (Asparagaceae) 63

Ficus (Moraceae) 64

Nerve Plant (Acanthaceae) 67

Pothos (Araceae) 68

Aquatic Plants **71**

Lucky Bamboo (Asparagaceae) 71

Marimo (Cladophoraceae) 72

ENVIRONMENTAL ZONES

Grouping the plants by the type of environment they desire allows beginning gardeners to get the feel of what a tropical or desert-type plant, for example, wants and needs. In your imagination, you can paint the stark desert landscape or lush rain forest where your plant would grow in the wild. Or perhaps your plant doesn't grow in soil at all, but rather makes its home in water. Most indoor plants fall into one of the following four categories, which you can use to guide your plant care.

DESERT PLANTS

Ah, the plants that thrive on neglect. Give this group bright, direct light, water them infrequently, and keep them out of drafts, and you will be rewarded. While cacti are perhaps what come to mind when you think of desert plants, this group includes palms and the colorful succulent echeveria.

TEMPERATE PLANTS

A group that includes such favorites as ferns, temperate plants tend to like consistent moisture but can tolerate low or filtered partial sunlight, making them good for pots or projects that won't sit right in front of windows. They're also not terribly finicky about temperature, making them versatile houseplants.

TROPICAL PLANTS

A popular category of houseplants that includes some showy beauties like the nerve plant and the Seussian dracaena, tropical plants exhibit a wider variety of lighting needs, from low to bright, but they all have this in common: they love humidity. These are the plants for people who love to mist, and they grow well in bathrooms and terrariums, anywhere the humidity is high and constant. Tropical plants crave warmer temperatures and like to dry out in the pot between watering.

AQUATIC PLANTS

No soil required, the species included here are all freshwater plants that are exceptionally easy to care for and excellent for beginners. They thrive in low light and need only an occasional change of their water and some fertilizer now and then.

DESERT PLANTS

From cacti to tillandsia, these are plants that don't like to be fussed over.

AIR PLANT (BROMELIACEAE)

A fantastic specimen that used to be hard to find, air plants, or tillandsia, are now carried in a wide variety of nurseries, online, and even in big-box garden centers. They grow wild in places like Florida and Mexico, where some people consider them pests. For the indoor gardener, they are anything but. These spiky, swirly, filament- or ribbonlike plants don't need a formal place to rest and can hang out most anywhere. They literally don't put down roots, as they lack them entirely. Instead, they use trichomes, minute scales on their leaves, to help them absorb moisture as well as nutrients from the air around them. This makes air plants excellent for beginners as well as for crafts or for tiny spaces. You don't even need a pot! As an added bonus, all air plants are nontoxic and won't hurt animals or kids who get ahold of one, though the plant might not fare well if they do.

Care and Feeding

Air plants like bright, filtered light and some airflow. Because they lack roots, they require specialized watering and feeding techniques. To water, depending on the humidity of your indoor environment, mist thoroughly at least twice a week or remove your air plant from its home and give it a soak in tepid water for no more than 20 minutes. Oversoaking an air plant is a common mistake and can drown the plant, causing it to die. After soaking, remove the plant, shake it, and allow it to dry upside down so water doesn't collect at the base of the leaves and cause rot. When misting, spray with enough water to cause the plant to darken slightly. To feed air plants, use a specialized foliar fertilizer (see Plants with Special Needs, page 31).

FAVORITES

The best way to shop for an air plant is to do it in person, perusing the myriad cool shapes, colors, and textures.

Tillandsia caput-medusae has spherical, wavy leaves thought to resemble the snakes emanating from the mythical Medusa's head.

A fuzzy species native to Ecuador, *T. tectorum* grows high in the mountains, where it sips water from the clouds.

CACTUS (CACTACEAE)

While the saguaro cactus, the tall species with "arms" straight out of an old western movie, might be the most iconic species in this group, this is a large family with plenty of diverse shapes and colors to choose from—and don't forget their beautiful yearly blooms! Not all cacti have fierce spines; in fact, some are delightfully fuzzy to the touch. Like most succulents, cacti store water in thickened parts of the plant. Rather than fleshy leaves, though, the cacti have specialized, fleshy stems (their spines are actually modified "leaves"). Many have texture on the stem as well—they might be ribbed or knobby or corrugated—which is another adaptation meant to help them conserve water. Chances are, your home is more hospitable than the Sonoran Desert, resulting in easy care and a happy cactus.

Care and Feeding

If you want to kill your cactus, overwater it. This is the most common reason people fail with this plant. Instead, allow your cactus to get bone dry between watering and make sure it's planted in cactus mix or a well-draining substrate with sand or rock. Water about every 3 to 6 weeks, depending on the humidity of your environment, giving it a drink when the soil feels completely dry to the touch. If the plant starts to shrivel, you are not watering frequently enough, while mushy spots are signs you've given too much moisture. Unsurprising for a desert plant, in order to be healthy, the cactus wants lots of light and thrives when it's bright and the temperatures are warm. If the light is too low, the cactus will go dormant rather than growing or flowering. If you keep the cactus in an office or someplace with less light, give it a sunny "vacation" every so often.

A ZEBRA BY ANY OTHER NAME

The plant commonly called the zebra cactus or zebra plant is not really a cactus at all but *Haworthia fasciata*, a cool, banded specimen of another type of succulent called the haworthia. These diminutive plants look like miniature aloes and make great indoor container plants. Don't allow water to sit in their rosettes, allow them to dry out thoroughly between watering, and keep them in bright but indirect light.

MOON CACTUS

FISHHOOK CACTUS

BALLOON CACTUS

ECHEVERIA (CRASSULACEAE)

One of the most iconic succulents, echeveria have gorgeous rosettes that are plumper and rounder than that of their cousin, sempervivum (page 53), and are as high maintenance as Victorian ladies. That said, they're worth it, showing off with colors from fierce to frosty to fiery and everything in between. What looks like a curvaceous flower on these plants is really a rosette of fleshy leaves mimicking the shape of roses, lotuses, and other true blossoms. While many people in warmer climates grow them outdoors, they work well inside, either displayed as solo specimens, grouped, or used for texture as part of a bowl or frame.

Care and Feeding

Echeveria want lots of light. If the plants don't get it, they will reach for the sun and get "leggy," stretching out to find the sun they crave. To keep them compact in form and the rosettes tight, keep the plants in bright, indirect light. Direct sunlight concentrated through a window or other glass could burn them, turning the plant white in affected spots. When it comes to watering, this prima donna does not like to be surprised, preferring to sip moisture rather than gulp it. Give your echeveria a regular watering routine for best results. Water in modest amounts, taking care to avoid getting water in the rosettes, and then leave alone for 2 to 4 days or until the plant has taken in the water. Top it off with a modest drink, then leave the plant alone until the soil dries out, about 2 weeks, before repeating the process. For hotter climates, check the plant weekly rather than biweekly. No matter what you do, don't allow water to remain inside the rosettes or the plant might rot. A regular application of bacterial inoculant is all it needs for food.

FAVORITES

With so many choices, it's hard to pick favorites! While I usually choose my echeveria by looks alone, these cultivars reward with unusual or distinctive colors:

Echeveria 'Black Prince' is a deep purple while *E.* 'White Rose' is ghostly pale and looks almost like a lotus flower.

E. 'Rainbow' is a variegated rosette that is barely ruffled, with rosy new growth.

E. 'Blue Curls' is cool toned and frilly.

PALM (ARECACEAE)

Both excellent air purifiers and graceful in form, palms make excellent indoor plants. Standing sentry in a corner or leaning over a chair or couch, palms add interest and movement to any room and some offer height as well. While many of us think of desert islands when we think of palms, in truth they come from a range of habitats, from dry desert landscapes to dense rain forests. Because of this, you'll want to take care to give your type of palm exactly what it needs. Because many palms, especially those popular as potted plants, come from drier climates, I have included them in this section.

Care and Feeding

Pay careful attention to your type of palm, as these plants' light needs run the spectrum from bright to filtered, though in general, palms will tolerate lower light than many people imagine, just not growing as quickly or producing as many fronds. Parlor palms are flexible and will tolerate even low light. Fan palms thrive in bright light while fishtails are happy in moderate to bright light. Watering, too, will depend on your type of palm. As a rule, palms aren't super finicky about the consistency of their watering and want to dry out between drinks. Overwatering and rot are a much greater risk than underwatering palms. Bimonthly feeding is enough to keep palms happy.

WHOA, THERE!

The jaunty ponytail palm (*Beaucarnea recurvata*) is a slow-growing plant distinctive for its bulbous base and upright shock of fronds resembling a ponytail. Interestingly, ponytail palms are not palms at all, but a type of succulent from the lily family, native to Mexico. This plant could better be called the camel palm, as its swollen base is used to store water, making the plant very drought tolerant and easy to care for. True palm or not, the ponytail palm is an excellent container plant requiring nothing more than bright light and occasional water.

SNAKE PLANT (ASPARAGACEAE)

The perfect plant for the "black thumb," the snake plant, also called (rather rudely) mother-in-law's tongue, really just wants to be left alone. Like, really. You can put this one just about anywhere, including some dim, forgotten corner, where it will proudly stand guard. Snake plants don't have to be (or want to be) watered or repotted often at all. In exchange for your neglect, you receive strong structural leaves that emerge from their pot like cobras being charmed out of a basket. Varieties range from light yellow-green to nearly black, with most edged in contrasting colors or even banded or striped. Snake plants give off oxygen mostly at night, making them a favorite choice for bedrooms.

Care and Feeding

Snake plants can be put just about anywhere. While they do enjoy some natural light, they will tolerate an all-fluorescent environment such as an office. Really the only thing you can do to kill a snake plant is to overwater it. Make sure the soil becomes thoroughly dry before watering and discard any water that accumulates in the tray. Most people find they go between 2 to 6 weeks between watering. The ideal vacation plant!

FAVORITES

Sansevieria trifasciata 'Hahnii', or bird's nest snake plant, is a low-growing dwarf cultivar with fun stripes that looks great on a tabletop.

S. cylindrica, or the African spear plant, has leaves curved in semicircular shapes.

S. trifasciata 'Twist', as the name suggests, sports leaves that twist and turn as they reach for the sky.

TEMPERATE PLANTS

This is the plant group for the moderates—no temper tantrums or difficult care here, though they do like a bit of attention.

FERN (POLYPODIACEAE)

A sprawling class of specimens that includes many old favorites of the houseplant world, ferns offer a range of textures in their fronds—the name for fern leaves—from thick and jagged to lacy and airy. Ferns are great choices for people who like to baby their plants because they love to be watered and misted. Putting them in a cloche or closed environment reduces their fussiness a bit, for those who want the same look with easier care.

Care and Feeding

In nature, ferns grow as part of the understory or attach themselves to bark or trees, depending on the species. This means most are used to dappled light and partial shade, making them great choices for low-light environments. The staghorn fern is one exception. It hails from tropical climates in Southeast Asia and Australia and wants bright but indirect light. At home in moist temperate or tropical rain forests and woodlands, ferns love humidity. Keep the soil around your fern moist to the touch, watering anywhere from daily to every couple of days. Once a week, give your fern a good misting and it will love you back! If the heat or air conditioning is often running in your home, take care to compensate for that drier air by paying more attention to your fern and watering more frequently.

FAVORITES

Tried-and-true Boston (*Nephrolepis exaltata* 'Bostoniensis') or Dallas (*N. exaltata* 'Dallasii') ferns offer the most classic fern look and relatively easy care.

The staghorn fern (*Platycerium bifurcatum*) is an unusual specimen in that it's an epiphyte, drawing moisture and nutrients from the air rather than by rooting in soil, which means it's an excellent fern for mounting and hanging on the wall (see Mounted Staghorn Fern, page 133).

FERN'S FRIEND, MOSS

Friends out in the wild, mosses and ferns make excellent companion plants in terrariums and bowls, each playing up the form of the other and needing similar care and feeding. Mosses come in two types: one grows in soil, the other on objects like rocks or branches. They come in a range of textures and colors and send up delicate little spores that can be quite cute. While mosses don't need a lot of light, they like to stay wet. Mosses that grow on objects rather than in soil should be misted daily.

PEACE LILY (ARACEAE)

FAVORITES

Spathiphyllum 'Mojo Lime' is a light, bright green and a fun variation on the standard deep-emerald leaf color.

S. 'Sensation' is one of the largest peace lilies, growing gorgeous rippled leaves that can measure 2 feet long!

S. 'Domino' sports white flecks and streaks on its dark leaves.

S. 'Little Angel' is perfect for small spaces and containers. A dwarf peace lily, it's easy to get to flower.

Not a true lily at all, the peace lily, or *Spathiphyllum*, is in the same family as the philodendron. It is popular both for glossy, deep-green leaves and attractive and distinctive white flowers, which are formed by a tubular spadix surrounded by the spathe, a "petal" that is really a modified leaf. If these plants have the right nutrients, they should shoot up flower stalks every few months, making for a rewarding specimen. For as pretty as they are, peace lilies are great plants for beginners. Don't water them enough, and they'll just sag and get droopy, telling you it's time. Once you give them a drink, they'll perk right up without holding a grudge.

Care and Feeding

Low to moderate light is best for these plants, as they will burn if placed in direct light. Though the peace lily is very demonstrative about its thirst, try not to let it get to the point of drooping, as it stresses the plant. That said, while it's a lot of work for most plants to recover from drying out too much, peace lilies are unusually hardy in this respect. Water weekly or when the soil becomes dry. As the peace lily is a flowering plant, you may need to supplement it with organic fertilizer (see Create Healthy Soil, page 30). If your peace lily hasn't flowered in a while, take that as a sign that the plant either needs to be repotted or needs some extra phosphorus.

SEMPERVIVUM (CRASSULACEAE)

A popular succulent for all the right reasons, sempervivum are hardy plants that come in shapes from rosettes to balls to globe artichoke look-alikes. Some look satiny, others spiky, and some even look like they're covered with spiderwebs. Commonly referred to as hen and chicks, the plants reproduce by sending up little babies (the "chicks"), which can be plucked off and made into new plants. Usually ranging from green to silvery in the winter months, they turn brighter colors in the spring and fall. Sometimes mistaken for their cousin echeveria, sempervivum cultivars are generally darker with sharper, faceted leaves and require very different care.

Care and Feeding

Sempervivum want moderate light, but they're not fussy. I've had good success placing them in a range of lighting conditions. Water when the soil dries out, about every 2 to 4 weeks. Sempervivum do better if you slowly and evenly saturate the soil rather than pouring water in a puddle on one side. As a mounding succulent, this plant naturally sheds the bottom layer of leaves as part of a normal process of growth. Don't misinterpret that as a sign that you are overwatering. Use bacterial inoculant once a quarter.

FAVORITES

Cobweb buttons (*Sempervivum arachnoideum*) has white filaments that stretch across the plant, looking ever so much like a spiderweb.

The cultivars S. 'Aglow', S. 'Red Ace', and S. 'Fuego' are but three of the brightly colored specimens that gleam in nearly jeweled tones.

BEGINNER'S CHOICE

In the same family (Crassulaceae) as sempervivum, both miniature and wavy varieties of jade plant (*Crassula ovata*) require the same care and also make excellent choices for indoor gardening. Sempervivum and jade plants are both tolerant and thus qualify as good beginners' succulents for use in projects or potted on their own.

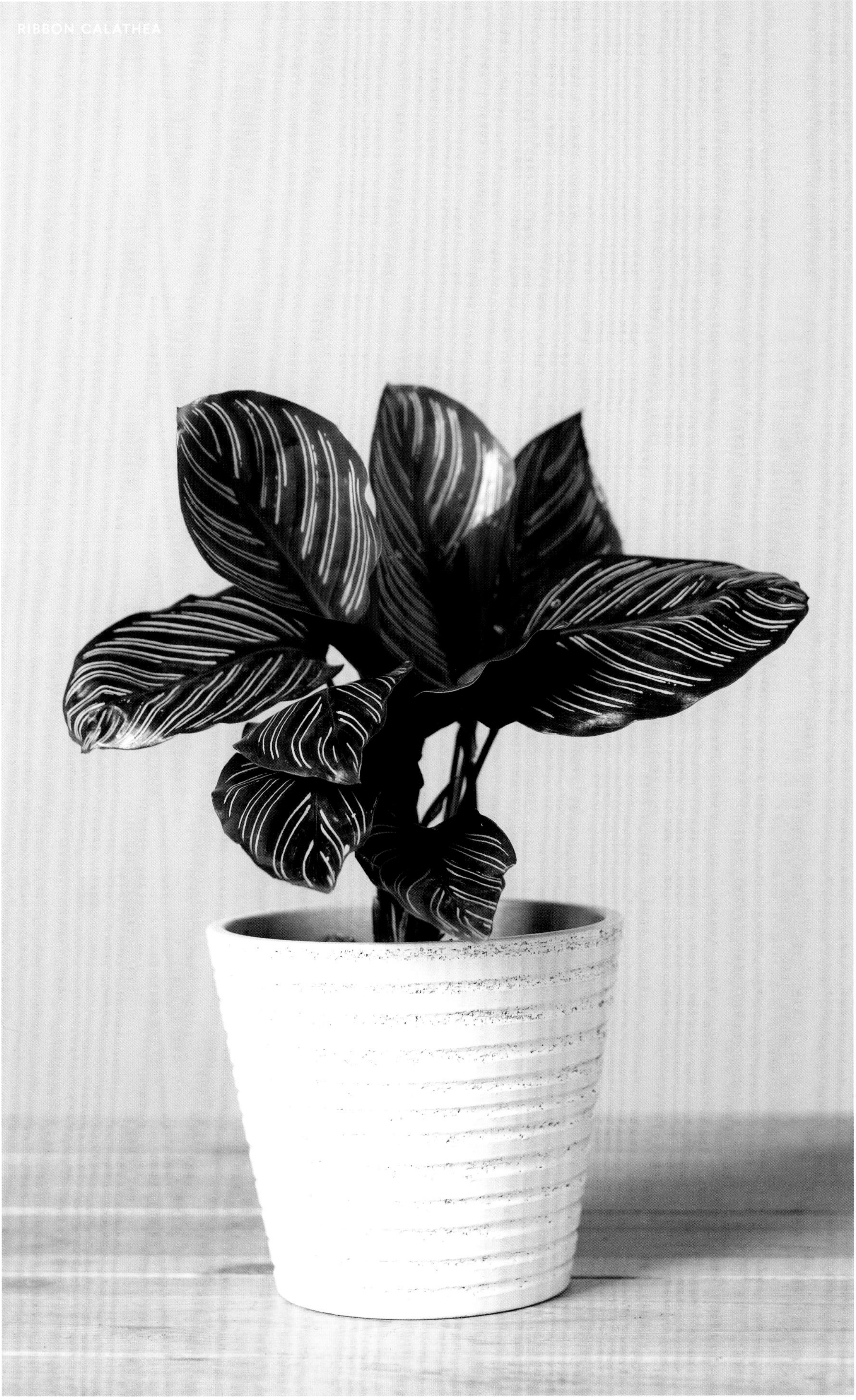
RIBBON CALATHEA

TROPICAL PLANTS

While not all of the plants in this group would be found in a tropical rain forest, they share a love of warmth and more consistent moisture.

CALATHEA (MARANTACEAE)

A type of tropical shrubbery, calathea have big, beautiful leaves that are so ornate they're downright flashy. This is a diverse group coming in lots of shapes and hues, though most have some type of marbling on the leaf that have earned them common names such as rattlesnake plant and peacock plant. They're also one of my favorite houseplants to give to people who have low-light environments, because they don't really want direct sun. Calathea are excellent plants for people who want drama without flowers.

Care and Feeding
Keep out of direct sun, as that could burn the leaves. Some species like bright, filtered light, though I find calathea will tolerate darker corners. Calathea are native to places like Brazil and want humidity and even moisture. Water weekly and mist every other day if your air is particularly dry or if you have a type that wants more humidity. Browning leaf edges mean the plant needs a more humid environment.

FAVORITES

Calathea rufibarba (also called feather plant or fuzzy feather) is one of my all-time favorite plants. The spear-shaped leaves are slightly ruffled, with deep-burgundy undersides. The best part: the leaves are covered with tiny hairs that make them feel like velvet.

C. orbifolia, a variety that requires more humidity, has large green leaves that are crinkled almost in an accordion fashion.

C. ornata sports jazzy pink stripes.

JUST LIKE A PRAYER

In the same family as calathea, *Maranta leuconeura*, or the prayer plant, earned its popular name because its leaves fold up and together at night. Perfect for beginning gardeners, the prayer plant has a low, spreading growth habit and nicely patterned leaves.

CAST-IRON PLANT (ASPARAGACEAE)

FAVORITES

Aspidistra elatior 'Milky Way' is a very unique cultivar. It's a solid bright green speckled with yellow dots that look just like the stars sprinkled in our galaxy. The leaves gently glow in low light.

A. elatior 'Snow Cap' has long, elegant leaves topped with caps of bright white.

A. ebianensis 'Flowing Fountains' is a smaller aspidistra whose glossy leaves shoot up from the center and gently slope, imitating water from a fountain.

If you inherited Grandma's cast-iron skillet, you'll appreciate how indestructible this appropriately named plant really is. In the same family as the snake plant, the cast-iron plant is like its leafier, harder-to-kill, super chill alter ego. For as easy as it is to grow, it's pretty: wide, sweeping leaves come off an elegant, narrow stem with new growth spreading through the soil, popping up new spears. But the real appeal comes from how forgiving it is. If you or someone you know is a serial plant killer, this is the one that will survive. It can take light but thrive with very little, can be root-bound or fill a pot, doesn't mind humidity but doesn't need it either. See what I mean?

Care and Feeding

Used as an outdoor plant, the cast-iron plant likes deep shade. While it prefers low light indoors, it's fairly tolerant of different conditions. Water weekly or whenever the soil becomes dry to keep your cast-iron plant happiest, and add bacterial inoculant to the water about once a quarter.

THE PLANT TO SURVIVE THE ZOMBIE APOCALYPSE

If you were going to have a contest for hardest to kill, snake plants and cast-iron plants might bow down to *Zamioculcas zamiifolia*, better known as the ZZ plant, often seen in commercial settings because it tolerates completely artificial light and can survive long periods without watering. In fact, the ZZ plant proves a disappointment to some gardeners because it doesn't noticeably grow or change much at all.

CITRUS (RUTACEAE)

There may be no more rewarding indoor edible than citrus, with its bright, glossy leaves, fragrant flowers, and juicy fruit. A natural for gardeners with indoor and outdoor spaces, potted citrus can grace a patio or balcony in the summer, lending an Italian Riviera kind of vibe. Once the weather cools, place it in a sunny window for a hit of summer all winter long. This is an excellent choice for goal-oriented gardeners. Growing citrus indoors is the most akin to outdoor vegetable gardening in two respects: one, you get to enjoy the (literal) fruits of your labor, and two, you need a bit more space plus a bright, sunny window where your tree can thrive.

Care and Feeding

Citrus trees want the same conditions that the fruit evokes—warmth, sun, light. As a minimum, you want the tree to receive 6 hours of direct sun per day, and a south-facing window is ideal. You can also speed up fruit production with grow lights or windowsill heat mats to provide warmth. It takes a lot of energy to make fruit, and it also makes a plant thirsty! Water your citrus daily or every other day, never allowing the soil to dry out for more than a day between drinks. That flowering and fruiting process also means that citrus needs more nutrients than some other plants. See Plants with Special Needs (page 31) for more information on feeding these cultivars.

FAVORITES

Mexican lime, or Key lime (*Citrus aurantiifolia* 'Swingle'), is the smallest of the limes and generally easier to grow than lemons, but Key lime trees do have thorns or spikes on their branches, so take care when plucking your fruit.

Moro blood orange (*C.* × *sinensis* 'Moro') is fun to grow for its dark-fleshed fruit. It tolerates colder temperatures than limes and can be dwarfed through pruning.

FRUIT COMES TO THOSE WHO WAIT

Citrus trees need to be at least 3 years old before they will bear fruit. If you are looking for immediate gratification, look for trees with fruit when you buy them or buy trees guaranteed to be "of age," and plant them in a pot that anticipates future growth. Once the tree produces its first crop, prune back any nonfruiting branches to encourage a compact growing habit and keep the tree focused (see Above the Soil, page 21). While you can grow any type of citrus indoors, trees labeled as dwarf varieties do best.

DIEFFENBACHIA (ARACEAE)

FAVORITES

Dieffenbachia maculata 'Tropical Tiki' is a big plant (up to 5 feet tall and wide!) with leaves speckled with green, yellow, and white. Showy and fun.

D. 'Camille' is a popular dwarf cultivar with green-edged leaves dominated by creamy centers.

D. 'Compacta' is a good choice for terrariums, as it stays small.

Like their cousin the peace lily, dieffenbachia have garnered legions of fans for their pretty leaves, tolerance of low light, and an ability to withstand some neglect. While their name may seem hard to pronounce (*dif-in-bawk-iya*), the common name—the dumb cane plant—hardly seems fitting for such a lovely specimen with leaves in a range of green hues often flecked with white. The common name does have a tale to tell, with many sources saying it refers to the toxic sap generated by the plant, which can irritate the mouth and throat and cause difficulty swallowing (or speaking, hence "dumb"). This makes this plant a good one to keep out of reach of pets and kids.

Care and Feeding

While dieffenbachia really love bright light, you can get away with sticking them in a corner. Different varieties have different tolerance for lighting conditions, but the beauty of this plant is that it is not likely to die from your mistake! Water weekly or when the soil becomes dry. As an herbaceous perennial, like all leafy plants, dieffenbachia appreciates a bit of extra nitrogen (see Create Healthy Soil, page 30).

DRACAENA (ASPARAGACEAE)

This group is one of the most diverse in the indoor plant world, so diverse that, put two dracaena side by side, and you might be hard-pressed to say they were related! Some grow tall on lanky stems, looking almost like trees out of a Dr. Seuss book. Others are more compact, with bushy bunches of wide, tapering leaves, and still others resemble bamboo (see Lucky Bamboo, page 71). They come in every color of green, some with spots, some with dots, others with stripes, and more. You can identify a dracaena by its growth habit, with new leaves sprouting from the top of a common stalk. What's more, dracaena are very forgiving houseplants, offering beginning gardeners uncommon range in style and form.

Care and Feeding

Low to medium light is best for most dracaena, and keep them out of direct sun. Water weekly or when the surface of the soil is dry, and use bacterial inoculant every other month.

FAVORITES

Dracaena deremensis 'Limelight' has electric spring-green leaves.

D. fragrans var. *massangeana*, a popular varietal commonly called corn plant, grows in a distinctive pattern with canes and leaves that resemble cornstalks. The leaves can be variegated or a solid green.

D. marginata, also called dragon tree, comes in attention-getting patterns. 'Tricolor' has leaves striped in red, green, and white, and 'Bicolor', in green and red.

FICUS (MORACEAE)

Iconic and handsome, ficus are very common as indoor plants, in spite of a deserved reputation for being downright difficult. Just *think* of moving or repotting an indoor ficus and it will throw a fit, dropping its leaves all at once like the needles on poor Charlie Brown's Christmas tree. That said, if you have a bright corner crying out for a graceful, leafy plant, then put a lovely ficus there and leave it. Ficus do need some space and don't like transitions, so start with a larger pot than the plant needs and let it grow into it. If your ficus does drop all its leaves? At least you know it's not you . . .

Care and Feeding

Keep ficus clear of direct sun but give them bright light and water weekly or biweekly, or just when the soil becomes dry. Some specimens, like the fiddle leaf fig, want moderate light and benefit from a dust of their leaves with a soft cloth and neem oil. Keep all ficus out of drafts or prepare for the shedding!

NERVE PLANT (ACANTHACEAE)

Ostensibly named for the visible yellow or white veining on each leaf resembling a branching nervous system, the nerve plant, or fittonia, also has some high anxiety, manifested as distinct likes and dislikes. The plants do like consistent moisture, making them excellent for terrariums, and they're great in hanging baskets because their natural form is orb shaped, making a neat ball. They dislike being transplanted or having their roots touched—their own nervous system is delicate!—and can suffer terribly from root shock. That said, nerve plants are worth the trouble, offering fascinating leaf patterns in pink or white, with dramatic, towering spikes of flowers that stick up from the foliage.

Care and Feeding

This plant prefers filtered light. If it is near a window, make sure you have at least a sheer curtain to protect it. As a rain forest plant, this guy likes to stay consistently moist. Water one to three times a week, depending on the humidity of your home, or make it lower maintenance by placing it in a bowl or terrarium to help conserve moisture. Water when the surface of the soil feels dry. Depending on how quickly your nerve plant grows, it may need more nutrients to help it along. Fast growers would enjoy monthly applications of bacterial inoculant. More slow-growing varieties can be fertilized every other month.

FAVORITES

There are many types of nerve plants, so choose a leaf pattern that really appeals to you.

Pink fittonia (*Fittonia albivenis*) have dark-green leaves with striking pink veining.

F. verschaffeltii var. *argyroneura* 'Minima' is more compact in form and great for bowls and terrariums.

F. albivenis 'Skeleton' sports glowing yellow-green leaves with bright-red veins.

POTHOS (ARACEAE)

If you've been searching for a rewarding plant that's nearly impossible to kill, look no farther. One of the most common houseplants, pothos, or devil's ivy as it's sometimes called, is a trailing vine with heart-shaped leaves that are variegated in hues of green, cream, and pale to bright yellow. It's a vigorous grower, which means that even beginning indoor gardeners can literally measure their success. If you don't have room for the pothos to sprawl more than 10 feet (really!), then you can either trim the vine or train it up walls, onto the ceiling, or around windows or pillars (see Vertical Vines, page 129).

Care and Feeding

Pothos do better with bright but indirect light, though they'll thrive in most lighting conditions. While they will tolerate very low light, their growth will not be as vigorous. More than light, it's the heat they are the most sensitive to—keep them away from direct sun. Water weekly and allow them to dry out between watering. These plants will tell you if they're thirsty and slump as though depressed. Water and see them perk right back up again.

AQUATIC PLANTS

While many plants will tolerate hydroculture, these plants eschew soil, making them some of the easiest houseplants to care for and enjoy.

LUCKY BAMBOO (ASPARAGACEAE)

What we call bamboo in the indoor plant world is really two different classes of plants. Lucky bamboo is not a true bamboo at all but a type of dracaena. You can tell lucky bamboo from its true bamboo cousin because it has a stalk that produces leaves from the top rather than shoots that come up from the soil—the kind you eat in your stir-fry. What makes lucky bamboo so easy is that it has only one criterion for staying happy: keep it wet. So long as you don't let it dry out, you have a fun, easygoing houseplant to bring you good fortune.

Care and Feeding

This hardy plant is used to filtered low light and that's what it likes best, though it will tolerate even office situations with fluorescent lighting. While you can plant lucky bamboo in soil, the best way to "plant" and keep it is in a watertight vessel with at least an inch of water in the bottom. Change out the water when it starts to get murky, and obey the cardinal rule: don't let your container run dry. If the plant has no access to water, you will see the top of the lucky bamboo start to die off, and at that point it is only a matter of time until you will need a new plant. For this reason, clear vessels make it easier to ensure the plant has enough water. About once a quarter, you'll need to add a drop of liquid fertilizer formulated for aquatic plants, usually high in nitrogen, to your container.

FAVORITES

Some lucky bamboo comes with intricately braided stalks or stalks trained into spirals that add extra interest and texture.

Dracaena sanderiana, or white ribbon, has lovely striped leaves.

MARIMO (CLADOPHORACEAE)

FAVORITES

Marimo (*Cladophora aegagropila*) don't come in different varieties or cultivars— they only come in different sizes— with larger (older) specimens costing more.

One of the only plants to be referred to as a "pet" or "friendly," marimo sink and float in their watery habitat in their quest for photosynthesis and gravitate toward one another, creating the illusion that these fuzzy balls are playing. Often billed as moss balls, these fascinating green spheres are actually balls of string algae that grow on the bottom of a select few lakes in the Northern Hemisphere, including in Iceland and Japan, where they are considered good luck.

Care and Feeding

Both adorable and easy, marimo can be kept in a variety of water temperatures but do best in cooler water that better mimics the environment of their lake homes. They can be housed in decorative vases or even just a cup of water so long as the water is changed out weekly. Marimo are a great addition to any fish tank as well, as, ironically, these algae balls help suppress the growth of pesky brown algae that tend to plague freshwater fish tanks. Although marimo are not particularly picky, they enjoy moderate, indirect light. If the outsides of the marimo become slimy, simply remove them from the container and gently squeeze—like you would wring out a sponge. These are very slow growers, averaging only about 2 centimeters a year! They are also very long lived, with the oldest recorded specimens over 100 years old.

III. PLANT
PROJECTS

I have hundreds of potted plants in my store, but the ones that immediately draw the customer's eye are the crafted plant projects. Whether it's a carefully sculpted underwater garden, a tillandsia perched in a gleaming geometric home, or a lush fern, artistically bound and seemingly suspended in air, plant crafts never fail to please. Try one or all of the curated projects that follow, and experience the same surprise and delight in your own space.

Terrariums and Bowl Gardens   79

Tropical Terrarium   81

Succulent Bowl   87

Hanging Air Plant Globe   93

Water Gardens   **97**

Marimo Habitat   99

Underwater Landscape   103

Floating Stems   109

Hanging and Vertical Gardens   113

Kokedama   115

Reflected Pyramid Himmeli   121

Vertical Vines   129

Mounted Staghorn Fern   133

The Kitchen Garden   **137**

Veggie Reincarnation   139

Living Herb Frame   149

TERRARIUMS AND BOWL GARDENS

As beautiful and as varied as the plant family you select, terrariums and bowl gardens are some of the most versatile formats for displaying your plant collection. Whether you pick striking cacti for a desertscape or construct a woodsy scene, bowl gardens and terrariums let you create a magical miniature world.

The first key to building a successful terrarium or bowl garden is to group together like plants that crave the same environment. Pair ferns and mosses with other plants that want high humidity, or combine drought-tolerant cacti with succulents and let dry out between watering. Completely enclosed terrariums are more appropriate for plants that need more moisture, and for that reason they are remarkably self-sustaining as the plants mature. Open-bowl systems require a bit more care since the moisture will evaporate into the air, but they are a better choice for plants that won't tolerate high humidity.

For both open bowls and terrariums, it pays to pack in your plants. Why? Plants grow to fit their environment. With less room to grow into, plants don't compete for resources like they do when given the option of open space. Planting more tightly not only adds texture and variety, but helps the plants keep their size consistent within the group.

Tropical Terrarium

This lush terrarium is packed with ferns, mosses, and other plants with variegated foliage, providing an array of green hues and cool textural contrasts. While a terrarium can be made in any glass container with a lid (I have one in a Turkish coffeepot!), here I chose a cloche, also known as a bell jar, which has a glass lid sitting on a fitted tray. Small garden or craft stores offer a variety of options, or find one online.

To make the terrarium, you'll also need a product called biochar, a nutrient-enhanced, pH-balanced charcoal used as a soil amendment and essential to balance the pH in terrariums. The biochar keeps the pH between 5.5 and 6.5, right where plants love it and mold and mildew don't! You can find biochar at specialty garden stores or online.

MATERIALS

- 1 (8-inch) glass cloche with lipped tray
- Biochar
- Pea gravel
- All-purpose potting soil
- 1 calathea (page 55), in 2½-inch pot
- 1 Boston fern (*Nephrolepis exaltata* 'Bostoniensis'), in 2½-inch pot
- 1 tiger fern (*N. exaltata* 'Tiger Fern'), in 2½-inch pot
- 1 creeping moss (*Vesicularia* species), in 2½-inch pot
- Decorative stones (optional)
- Bacterial inoculant

STEPS

1 Place the cloche in front of you and remove the top. Set aside. Cover the bottom of the cloche with a layer of biochar ¼ inch thick.

2 Add gravel to cover the biochar up to a maximum depth of about 1½ inches. If you want to create more height in your terrarium, use the gravel to build up a hill or slope.

3 Mound potting soil to a maximum depth of 3 inches on top of the gravel in the center of the cloche, allowing a ½-inch buffer (at minimum) of exposed gravel all the way around the circumference of the tray. Mounding the soil gives your plants more height and allows the cloche lid to rest on the gravel rather than on the soil. This keeps the lid clean and allows you to water the terrarium without removing it.

4 Remove the plants from their plastic pots and gently loosen the roots with your fingers, removing as much soil as possible. If the plants are root-bound, refer to Below the Soil (page 24) and trim them back. Take extra care when handling the moss, as mosses have very delicate root systems.

5 Push the calathea's roots into the center of the mound, far enough in to stabilize the plant. It's okay when planting to go deep, even if the roots hit the gravel, as plants will create new roots to grow into the soil. Plant the ferns immediately to the sides of the calathea. Gently break the moss into three sections and then surround the calathea and ferns with the moss. If any of the plants seem unstable, you can use stones to stabilize them, either as a design element or on a temporary basis until the plants root. Remember that the plants will continue to grow and fill out the space, so don't be concerned if it doesn't look too full at this point.

6 Mist the plants heavily with water with bacterial inoculant added; add a bit of water to the gravel as well. Place the cloche lid on the tray to cover the plants.

7 Place the completed terrarium in bright light for about a week. Foliage plants often experience transplant shock. Both the bacterial inoculant and the extra light will help the plants weather the first, crucial 72 hours. After that time, plants usually begin to bounce back. Once established, place in moderate, indirect light.

CARE: I do a visual check of terrariums once a week. Look for droopy plants and mosses or ground covers that look and feel dry. Add water by pouring it into the gravel rimming the edge of the tray. If you see condensation within a day after watering, leave the lid off the cloche for a few hours or even overnight to allow some moisture to evaporate. If there is too much moisture, terrariums get cloudy. A well-composed closed-loop system is very self-sufficient. Your mature terrarium might need watering only every couple of weeks to couple of months. Rotate your terrarium often so that the plants grow symmetrically and don't have to reach for light.

WATERING DOESN'T HAVE TO BE A CHORE

We all mean to be good plant parents, but sometimes life gets in the way, and then watering ends up feeling like one more item on our to-do list. If you notice your poor specimens going limp, you can avoid the shame (and stress on your plants) by changing how you *feel* about watering. I recommend using a beautiful or whimsical watering can or mister that you like to look at and will set out in your home. Just this simple switch can change watering from a chore into meditative time you look forward to.

VARIATION: CREATE A CUSTOM TERRARIUM

To create your own custom terrarium, choose plants that like humidity and try to cover the entire surface area of the soil with plantings. You can arrange your plants symmetrically so that it looks identical from all angles. It's also fun to make your terrarium look different from all sides. Mix and match taller plants to top the mounded soil, then surround with creeping or low-growing plants.

Center

You will want to choose a plant that has some height before the foliage begins.

Best picks:
- Mini palm (page 44)
- Dwarf dieffenbachia (page 60)
- Calathea (page 55)

Sides

Pick plants that will not grow too tall or that sprawl.

Best picks:
- Creeping Charlie (*Glechoma hederacea*)
- Creeping Jenny (*Lysimachia nummularia*)
- Nerve plant (page 67)
- Club moss (*Lycopodium* species)
- Miniature fern (page 49)
- Wandering Jew (*Tradescantia pallida*)

Ground Cover

The more plants in your terrarium, the easier the long-term care, as they'll work together to make a self-sustaining environment. Instead of live plants, you can plant seeds on the sides of your mound to help close up space.

Best picks:
- Grass or clover seed (*Trifolium* species)
- Moss spores, such as cushion moss (*Leucobryum* species)
- Baby's tears (*Soleirolia soleirolii*)
- Dichondra (*Dichondra micrantha*)—a ground cover that looks like mini lily pads!

Succulent Bowl

These gorgeous bowls are all about structure. Succulents are a varied family, including dramatic cacti, ponytail palm, and the seductive whorls and rosettes of echeveria or sempervivum. This simple-to-make but striking project really highlights the textural leaves of these plants. Sculptural and hardy, this project would make a great coffee-table focal point or could sit next to a sunny window. Or group your bowls to show off architectural containers and plants.

MATERIALS

- 1 (5-inch) container, made of any material except plastic, with or without drainage hole
- Nonporous substrate, such as pea gravel or bark
- Well-draining potting soil or cactus mix
- 7 to 10 succulents of varying heights, in 2½-inch pots
- Stones, decorative sand, or aquarium gravel to fill in open spaces (optional)
- Bacterial inoculant

TIP: If you water on the generous side, a concrete or terra-cotta pot will help absorb excessive moisture and give your plants a bit more cushion from sitting in soggy soil.

STEPS

1 With your container in front of you, layer in the bottom
  enough nonporous substrate to come one-third of the way
  up the side. If your container does not have a drainage hole,
  make sure this layer is substantial.

2 Using a spoon or your hand, add enough potting soil to form
  a layer no less than 1 inch and no more than 3 inches deep,
  depending on the size and depth of your container. If your soil
  layer is too thick, it will create too fertile of an environment
  and encourage competition among the plants. Your finished
  bowl should have substrate, soil, and air in about equal
  proportions.

3 Remove each succulent from its pot and, using your fingers,
  thoroughly remove as much soil as possible from the roots.
  With most succulents you can be fairly aggressive during this
  step. The benefit of removing the old soil is that it exposes the
  roots to their new environment and allows them to get over
  transplant shock more quickly.

4 Arrange your succulents in the bowl, planting just deeply
  enough that they stand up. I like to choose a taller specimen
  as the main focal point and place it slightly off center.
  Surround the focal point with three to five plants of medium
  height. Place low-growing succulents around the edges. Top off
  with soil as necessary, making sure the soil comes no higher
  than ¼ inch below the rim of your container to avoid spillover
  during watering.

5 If there is any exposed surface area after the plants are in,
  cover the spots with decorative rocks or stones, or any other
  nonporous material. Your bowl will be more successful if you
  plant in clusters and cover exposed soil rather than spreading
  out your plants.

6 Water with bacterial inoculant and place in bright light for a
  few days to minimize transplant shock.

CARE: If the container you choose does not have a drainage hole, you will need to water more sparingly as well as more frequently. Place succulent bowls in bright light to ensure they don't get leggy; echeveria and cacti especially prefer lots of sunlight, which in turn produces brighter colors in the plants. See Part II: Plant Guide (page 32) for detailed care instructions on your type of succulents.

BEST PICKS:

DROUGHT-TOLERANT PLANTS	PLANTS THAT NEED INFREQUENT WATERING
Cactus (page 40)	Jade plant (page 53)
Sempervivum (page 53)	Echeveria (page 43)
Snake plant (page 47)	String of pearls (*Senecio rowleyanus*)
Haworthia (page 40)	

VARIATION: CREATE A CACTUS BOWL

Depending on the cactus species you choose, make sure you wear gloves to protect yourself from thorny spines and handle the plants lightly.

MATERIALS

- 1 (3- to 5-inch) container, made of any material except plastic, with or without a drainage hole
- Gravel
- Cactus mix or a blend of half potting soil and half sand
- 5 to 7 cacti of varying heights, in 2½-inch pots
- Stones, decorative sand, or aquarium gravel to fill in open spaces (optional)
- Bacterial inoculant

STEPS

1 For a bowl using plants that like an arid environment, such as cacti, drainage is critical. Fill your container with a layer of gravel no less than 1 inch thick, or deeper if your container will allow it.

2 Remove the plants from their pots and use your finger to brush off any loose dirt; handle them very carefully and be gentle. Aggressive handling of the cactus or cactus roots can cause cactus rot, which could kill your plant. Better to leave some soil on the roots than be too aggressive.

3 Arrange your cacti in the bowl, planting just deeply enough that they stand up. Choose a taller specimen as the main focal point and place it slightly off center, then surround with medium and low-growing plants.

4 Top off with soil as necessary, making sure the soil comes no higher than ¼ inch below the rim of your container to avoid spillover during watering.

5 Place the finished bowl in a bright location for at least a week to help the plants get over transplant shock. For display, the bowl will do best if placed in direct sun.

Best picks:

- Golden barrel
- Peruvian old man (page 40)
- Pineapple (*Mammillaria longimamma*)
- Thimble (*M. gracilis* var. *fragilis*)
- Fishhook (page 40)
- Silver torch (*Cleistocactus strausii*)
- 'Ming Thing' (*Cereus validus* f. *monstrose*)

Hanging Air Plant Globe

If you're not already infatuated with air plants, this project will make you fall in love: it's a snap to make and care for, and the look is unique. These funky plants come in a range of spiky, swirling, sculptural styles, resembling everything from miniature octopi to Medusa to the Muppet Animal's gravity-defying hair.

MATERIALS

- 1 or more air plants (tillandsia, page 39)
- 1 open glass ball ornament (available in craft stores, some nurseries, and online)
- Nonporous decorative substrate, such as sand, gravel, or colored pebbles (optional)
- Shells, stones, or other decorations (optional)
- String or monofilament, for hanging
- Hardware, for hanging (optional) (see Hanging Your Globe, page 94)

STEPS

1 Mist the air plant or soak it in a bowl of water for 10 to 20 minutes. Make sure you remove the plant after no more than 20 minutes or else you might drown the plant. Remove it and tilt it upside down to make sure no water gathers at the base of the leaves. Allow to dry.

2 Place the orb on your worktable with the opening facing you. Add a layer of the decorative substrate, if desired. Since the plant doesn't need it, add as much or as little as you like.

3 Add your air plant (3a) as well as any decorations (3b). Make sure the air plant is easy to remove for watering.

4 Tie your string onto the loop and hang using the hardware, or tie on to an existing surface.

CARE: For ease of watering and fertilizing, remove your air plant from its orb. See page 39 for detailed instructions on caring for tillandsia.

HANGING YOUR GLOBE

People often ask about how to hang their air-plant projects once they're complete. Because they're so lightweight, there are a range of options. You can use a curtain or tension rod, L-brackets, or an eyebolt screwed directly into the ceiling. A sturdy and attractive branch also works, either propped against a wall or affixed to the wall or ceiling with screws and anchors, with the orbs tied onto the branch with string or monofilament. Embroidery hoops hung from the ceiling, from which the orbs then hang, create a mobile feel. Because of the delicacy of the plants and the glass spheres, you can group the orbs to create more of a statement piece.

WATER GARDENS

Fish optional, water gardens require a bit more outlay in terms of equipment and setup but are easy to maintain afterward. They also remove the most troubling of all beginning gardeners' questions: How much do I water? I also love water gardens for the vibrant bit of life they bring to a tabletop, a desk, or a darker corner. Water gardens that have water pumps or circulators also are very meditative; you can watch the gently undulating plants while you're soothed by the running water. But you don't need a tank or equipment for aquaculture, the formal name for raising plants in water. Sometimes, it's as easy as plopping a plant into a watertight vessel.

One of the most common issues with water gardens is algae buildup, and there are two easy ways to combat it. First, algae need light to thrive. Moving your water garden to a lower-light environment should help. If it doesn't, you can always turn to your friend the aquatic snail. Tiny, unobtrusive, fun to watch, and excellent at mowing down algae, they're an eco-friendly way to remove the murkiness and let your plants shine.

To source plants for water gardens, look in garden centers that stock plants for ponds or fountains, or in aquarium or fish-supply stores.

Marimo Habitat

Literally the just-add-water of the indoor plant world, this project is perfect for those nervous about under- or overwatering, since it throws the whole question out the window. Rather than soil, these minimalist arrangements use water as the growing medium for the plant, in this case marimo, a fuzzy, green little aquatic ball. Make sure to use a clear vessel so you can watch your marimo rise and fall and bob about.

MATERIALS

- 1 clear watertight container
- Colored gravel, pebbles, or substrate
- 1 to 3 marimo (page 72)
- Decorative rocks

STEPS

1 Cover the bottom of the container with at least an inch of gravel. This is not necessary but will help hide any sediment and keep the look clean.

2 Add the marimo onto the stones, and add decorative rocks if desired.

3 Fill the container with as much water as you like (the marimo just needs to stay wet), running the water over the back of a spoon to dissipate the flow and keep it from displacing the gravel. Try to keep the container in a place where the water won't warm up too much, out of direct light. The marimo will reproduce by splitting off new balls. Don't tear your marimo in half—the plant needs to birth the new marimo on its own.

CARE: Algae grow in water that is warm and exposed to light. To keep algae from building up, change out the water every 1 to 2 weeks. You can either carefully pour off the water from the vessel, using a strainer to catch the stones, or use a turkey baster to siphon the water out. If you do experience algae buildup, consider adding an aquatic snail or two from a pet store. Though fertilizer is not strictly necessary, encourage growth by burying an organic substrate fertilizer pellet in the gravel once every few months.

Underwater Landscape

Anyone who's ever paused to enjoy the look and sound of a fish tank will appreciate the soothing qualities of this underwater landscape with the gently bubbling water and diversity of foliage.

For the plants, cuttings are a good way to go, as they're less expensive and almost always root. Some stores, like Urban Sprouts (see Resources, page 185), sell cuttings, as will many aquarium supply companies, both brick-and-mortar and online. Adding petrified wood or stones to your tank creates the look of an underwater scene. I like to include special rocks I've picked up on beaches or on walks during vacation.

MATERIALS

- 1 (5-gallon) fish tank
- Washed pea gravel
- Aquarium substrate (Gro Pro is a good brand)
- 10 to 15 aquatic plant starts with varying growth habits
- Decorative rocks or petrified wood, rinsed in hydrogen peroxide and dried (optional)
- 1 water filter
- 1 water pump or bubbler

STEPS

1 Place the tank in front of you on a stable surface. Add a ½-inch layer of pea gravel to the bottom of the tank. If you want to sculpt any hills or mountains, do so now. Add a 1-inch layer of aquarium substrate. Different from gravel, substrate has nutrients in it that will help your plants thrive.

2 Place any cleaned rocks or other decorative items in your tank. Now arrange your plants, poking their roots through the substrate and into the gravel as necessary. I like to create one focal point and work outward. Make sure the taller plants are toward the back and that ground covers have some room to travel and sprawl. Place your plants close together, as close as you can without crowding. Though it may seem counterintuitive, this helps the plants form a self-sustaining ecosystem as they mature, since no one plant will compete for resources. Trim the roots of any plants that seem out of balance with the others. In general, aquatic plants aren't delicate and you can be fairly aggressive with their root systems. Because they don't suffer from transplant shock, they are usually quite successful.

3 If there are any empty spaces on the bottom of the tank after the plants are in, cover with gravel. Leaving the substrate exposed can make the tank cloudy.

4 When filling the tank, run the water over the back of a spoon to diffuse the water so that it doesn't disturb the bottom. The tank may become cloudy after filling, but it should settle after an hour or two. Follow the manufacturer's instructions to install the filter and pump.

CARE: Because of this tank's size, I've recommended a pump or bubbler to keep rot at bay. If you have a smaller tank, you can get away without one, though you'll need to change the water weekly to keep it fresh and cool. A turkey baster works very well for this! For tanks with pumps, every 2 weeks, swap out about 20 percent of the water in the tank for fresh water. If there is any algae present, try reducing the light the tank is exposed to or add aquatic snails to control it. Once every couple of months, fertilize with substrate pellets or tablets. If any of your plants are getting unruly, trim them back (see Above the Soil, page 21) and use the cuttings to cover a bald spot or give to a friend. Cuttings from aquatic plants nearly always root easily.

BEST PICKS:

Water sprite (*Ceratopteris thalictroides*)

Narrow leaf and XL Java fern (*Microsorum pteropus*)

Java moss (*Vesicularia dubyana*)

The heavily textured *Anubias barteri* var. *coffeefolia*

Dwarf baby tears (*Hemianthus callitrichoides* 'Cuba') as a low ground cover

Bucephalandra 'Green Wavy'

Cryptocoryne species

Eleocharis acicularis 'Mini'

Hygrophila pinnatifida

Pennywort

Dwarf *Potamogeton gayi*

Proserpinaca palustris

GIVE YOUR PLANTS SOME COMPANY

Though plants are the focal point here, you can certainly add fish to your tank. If you have a smaller tank with no pump or filter, you'll want to stay with bettas or tetras. General guidelines are that every inch of fish needs a minimum of 1 gallon of water, so don't overload your tank. Before adding fish, make sure you do your research or talk to the people who you buy them from, and don't get a type that eats plants! Avoid nibblers like guppies, for example. Cichlids including red zebra, cobalt and electric blue, and electric yellow lab do well and look festive.

Floating Stems

While this is one of the simplest projects in the book, in the interest of full disclosure, this is a high-maintenance indoor plant, making the arrangement nice for the short-term rather than a permanent addition to your home. Think dinner-party centerpiece or entryway conversation starter. That said, it's incredibly beautiful, just duck-lettuce stems floating gracefully in the water. While the plant features foliage and sometimes a flower above, the true focus is its feathery moorings below. As it needs cool water, make sure it's not in direct sun. As a variation on duck lettuce, you can substitute any plant in the lily pad family and follow the same steps.

MATERIALS

- 3 duck lettuce (*Pistia stratiotes*)
- 1 clear vessel, tall enough to fully submerge the roots underwater (at least 4 inches high)
- Organic liquid fertilizer for aquatic plants

STEPS

1 Depending on how the duck lettuce was grown, the roots might have soil clinging to them. Gently rinse them under running water and use your snips to clip off any mushy or unattractive spots.

2 Fill the vessel with clean, cool water, and add a drop of fertilizer.

3 Place your duck lettuce in the water. Place in bright light but avoid direct sun.

CARE: Pond plants eat nutrients out of the water, so they require monthly liquid fertilizer. As it's used to high-humidity environments, duck lettuce will also want to be misted daily. Remove any leaves that aren't doing well immediately and wipe the leaves every couple of days with a damp cloth. Every week, use a turkey baster to change out at least 20 percent of the water to keep it cool and fresh.

HANGING AND VERTICAL GARDENS

Everyone can bring plants indoors, even when floor space is at a premium. That's because just like plants outdoors—where vines tumble along fences or climb buildings, and where plants seed themselves in unlikely crevices and cracks or attach themselves to trees—indoor plants don't have to be confined to a tabletop. Remember that your home is a three-dimensional space, with walls and ceilings available. The projects in this section take advantage of the plants' natural tendencies to explore and give your plants a lofty place to perch. What's more, elevating plants creates more visual interest and allows you to highlight design, drawing the eye with shape, texture, and contrast. These projects are also an excellent way to brighten up dead corners and blank walls or make thoughtful homemade gifts.

Kokedama

Kokedama is a rustic, organic form that frees your plants from the rigid confines of a pot. These sensual, sculptural plantings (just a bound soil-and-moss container) originated in Japan before sweeping the United States. Literally translating as "moss ball," kokedama borrows several techniques from the art of bonsai and involves binding the roots of your chosen plant with sheet moss and string, then hanging it. As the plants grow, they sense the air surrounding the moss and interpret that boundary. Not only does that mean no repotting (ever!), but rather than focusing energy on putting down roots, the plants can concentrate on putting out leaves, fruit, and flowers for you to enjoy.

While some kokedama involve packing the ball with clay before adding moss, this is an easier method that's just as successful. More than just beautiful, kokedama are incredibly versatile and can be made with many types of plants. While this project uses a fern, as you become more comfortable with the technique, you can get creative. Before choosing your plant, think about where the finished project will hang. Low-light plants that crave humidity could hang above a tub or in your shower, while plants that want sun and more sun would love to be situated near a bright window. Also, while a variety of plant sizes will work, the more established the plant, the better it will do. I suggest using plants that come in a 6-inch pot or larger.

MATERIALS

- 4 (4-foot) pieces of string, plus 8 to 12 feet for wrapping
- 3 (2-ounce) packages of sphagnum moss sheets, such as SuperMoss brand
- 1 button fern, in 6-inch pot
- Monofilament, for hiding the string (optional) and hanging (about 5 feet)

STEPS

1 Take the four pieces of string and tie them together in the middle using a simple knot. Spread out the string so it radiates out from the center knot like a spiderweb.

2 Remove the moss from the packages and spread the sheets out in a mat on top of the string, centered, making the mat about 1 inch thick and the size of a dinner plate. You need enough moss to completely enclose the root system of your plant.

3 Remove the fern from its pot, retaining the soil around the roots. This is the one time you don't want to remove the old soil! If the plant looks root-bound, with roots circling at the bottom, trim them (see Below the Soil, page 24). Retain any soil that comes off when trimming the roots.

4 Place the root ball of your fern in the middle of your "plate," with the plant upright. Add back any loose or lost soil and pack it gently around the roots.

5 Now take the ends of one string and wrap the string across your plant's roots like a seat belt, securing each end with a firm knot to the center knot underneath the moss. Repeat with the remaining pieces of string. In the end, your fern should look like it's sitting in a bird's nest of moss.

6 Cut several additional pieces of string that are 3 to 4 feet in length. Tie one onto any of the "seat belts" you created in the last step and begin to wrap the string around the root ball like you would wrap a ball of yarn. Start packing in extra moss as needed to cover bare spots, adding string and wrapping in an elliptical fashion to round the ball and create a lush, even layer. Keep the string taut as you go and knot the strings tightly at every junction. Keeping the string taut is one of the most difficult parts of the project, but it is critical to the integrity of the finished project.

7 If you don't want to see the string, cut 4-foot lengths of monofilament, and repeat step 6, adding in another layer of moss and securing it with monofilament until the string is hidden. Knot the monofilament very tightly.

8 Tie monofilament onto the ball for hanging.

CARE: To water, take your kokedama down and give the ball
a soak in tepid water in a sink, bucket, or bowl for about 30
minutes. Allow it to dry briefly before rehanging. The frequency
of soaking will depend on the season. During hotter, drier
times, you might want to soak it twice a week, while weekly will
suffice when temperatures are more moderate. Adding bacterial
inoculant to the soaking water once a month will provide steady
fertilization that slowly tapers its nutrients (see Create Healthy
Soil, page 30).

BEST PICKS:

Any variety of fern (page 49)

Calathea (page 55), such
as peacock plant (*Calathea
makoyana*) or *C. orbifolia*

Dracaena (page 63)

Norfolk pine (*Araucaria
heterophylla*) seedlings

STRING CHOICES FOR KOKEDAMA

You have a couple of options for wrapping your kokedama, each contributing
to a different design look and level of upkeep. I don't recommend synthetic
yarns, as the dyes can leach into the plant's habitat. The most common
choices are:

- Natural string (such as cotton or jute), which preserves the quality of the
  soil, but you must rewrap every so often, as it eventually breaks down. This
  gives the most rustic look.
- Monofilament (fishing line), which provides the cleanest look and is also
  used to wrap over either natural or synthetic strings to compact and form
  the ball.

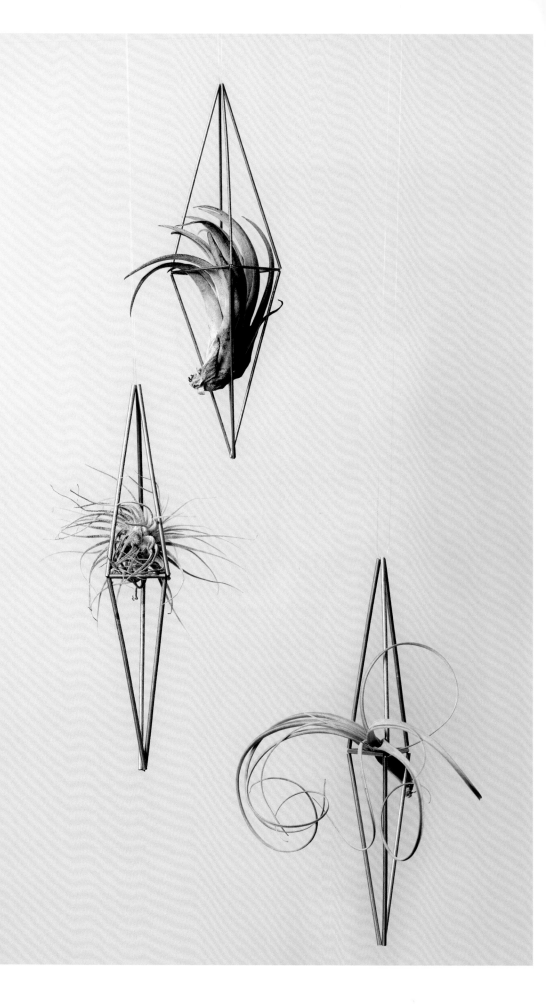

Reflected Pyramid Himmeli

Himmeli, a traditional woven ornament, remains popular in many Nordic countries as well as in the United States. I remember them adorning our Christmas tree when I was growing up, woven in intricate shapes out of golden straw. The word *himmel* in Swedish translates as "sky" or "heaven" and captures the delicate beauty of the geometric shapes and the way they seem to float on light and air. Taking an heirloom from generations past and recreating it in brass gives these lovely crafts a modern refresh and provides a unique perch for easy-care air plants. Because himmeli weigh almost nothing, they are a great choice for hanging in apartments or offices where you can't put in obtrusive hardware, or from ceilings that won't hold much weight. Even a thumbtack will hold them!

For materials, you will need to find waxed upholstery thread, as it is the only option stiff enough to make the weaving simple and yet keep it light; it has good surface tension and is easier to work with. While some people create himmeli using monofilament, I find it's slippery and difficult, especially for beginners, and also unnecessary, as you don't really see the thread in the finished project. Etsy.com is a good place to source precut brass himmeli tubes; the shop Yakutum has a variety of lengths and ships fast.

MATERIALS

- 4 (50-millimeter-long) ⅛-inch-diameter brass himmeli tubes
- 8 (100-millimeter-long) ⅛-inch-diameter brass himmeli tubes

- 1 spool of waxed upholstery thread
- One air plant (tillandsia, page 39)
- Hanging hardware (optional)

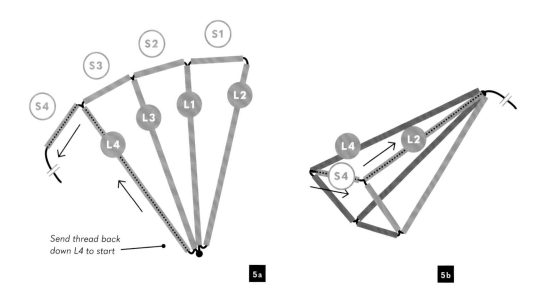

Send thread back down L4 to start

5a   **5b**

5 Add a long tube (L4) followed by a short tube (S3), then pass
   the thread back up the adjacent long tube (L3). If the project
   gets loose at any point, just tug on the thread and it will
   tighten up. Now you should have four long sides. You need to
   add the fourth short bottom edge. With the project lying flat,
   send the thread down through the most recently added long
   edge, and add the final short tube (S4) (step 5a). Go back up
   the opposite outside long edge (L2). You should now be able
   to fold the tubing into a four-faceted pyramid (5b).

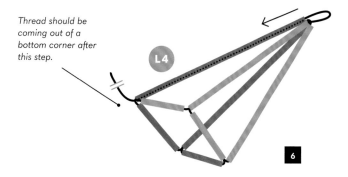

Thread should be coming out of a bottom corner after this step.

6

6 Thread back down through the adjacent long edge and inspect
   your himmeli. Every junction needs to have thread going
   through it to keep it tight.

7 The thread should now be hanging out of one long segment.
  Before adding on any more segments, you need to turn
  (never cross the street!). Put the thread through either of the
  adjacent short tubes.

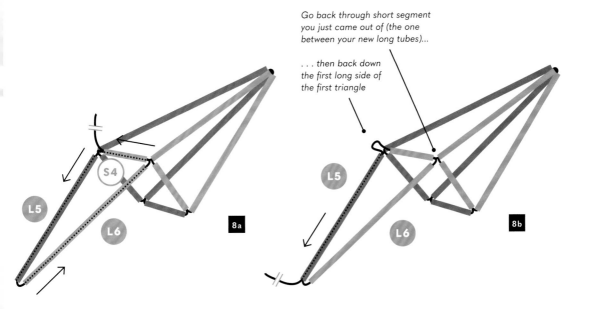

*Go back through short segment
you just came out of (the one
between your new long tubes)...*

*. . . then back down
the first long side of
the first triangle*

8 Add two long tubes (L5 and L6) to make your first reflective
  triangle (step 8a). Go back through the same short segment
  (S4) you just came out of, then back down the first (long) side
  (L5) of the triangle you just made (step 8b). While it seems
  like a lot of backtracking, in this style of weaving that's what
  creates strength.

Vertical Vines

Some of the most iconic outdoor plants are porch- and wall-climbing classics like grape, wisteria, clematis, and ivy. For some indoor gardeners, healthy vines like pothos can become a nuisance as they tumble off tabletops and reach across the floor, seeking new space to grow. I don't find the trailing habit of these plants a problem; rather, I use their superpower to create indoor installations that defy gravity and add color and texture to dead corners and boring spaces. In your bedroom, have a philodendron frame the window and your view outside. Or subdivide your space with orderly rows of adjacent plants that climb up walls and across the ceiling. While you can use bendable wire if you want to create a topiary shape, natural fibers provide the plant with a bit more natural traction if you are working with straight lines.

For beginning gardeners, this is also a very rewarding effort. Plants like pothos and ivy are fast growers, and you'll see your project begin to take shape very quickly. Pothos also tolerate low light, making vertical vines an option even for hallways, dark corners, or offices.

MATERIALS

- 1 trailing plant, in a 12-inch or larger pot
- 1 wooden stake (optional)
- Brass or clear thumbtacks
- Jute, twine, or monofilament

STEPS

1 Situate your pot and plan for future growth. As the plant climbs, you will need to provide it with a solid foundation and something to grip onto. For vines that might need extra support, insert a wooden stake into the pot and gently wind the tendrils around the stake. This will give the plant stability as it transitions from soil to another surface.

2 For one single vine, you can train it as you go, placing thumbtacks in a slightly zigzagging pattern to hold the plant to the wall and guide it where you want it to go. This is the simpler and less obtrusive of the options.

3 Alternatively, you can insert thumbtacks and then weave the string between them, placing string wherever you want to train the plant to go.

4 Whichever you choose, make sure you place your plant in a semipermanent location. Provide the first supports near the soil or the wooden stake to give the plant a sturdy perch from which to climb.

5 If it becomes necessary, trim your plant to keep its shape or to promote the growth of certain tendrils (see Above the Soil, page 21).

CARE: Depending on the plant you choose, provide moderate to low light. Some plants, like pothos, do not like extreme heat and shouldn't be placed in direct sun. Water weekly or when the soil becomes dry to the touch. Add an organic fertilizer with nitrogen to give an extra boost to the vine.

BEST PICKS:

Pothos (page 68)

Ivy (for bright-light locations)

Heart-leaf philodendron (*Philodendron hederaceum*) (for bright-light locations out of full sun)

Mounted Staghorn Fern

Capture an updated lodge look by forgoing the hunting trophies and instead hanging a lovely, living staghorn fern. These architectural beauties are native to the tropics, where they spring from crevices and the crooks of trees, soaking in nutrients through their fronds. This "air-drinking" habit—and their striking resemblance to a rack of antlers—makes staghorn ferns naturals for affixing to a slab of wood or bark and adorning your wall.

For the project, you can use any type of nail you like—such as galvanized or brass—so long as the nails have heads (i.e., are not finishing nails), as the nails will be used to hold the string fastening the fern to the hanging plaque.

MATERIALS

- 1 staghorn fern (page 49), in 6-inch pot
- 1 (7-inch-diameter or larger) bark or wood slab
- 2 D-hooks, for hanging
- Picture wire, for hanging (for curved bark mounts)
- 4 ounces sphagnum moss (such as SuperMoss brand)
- 12 to 25 (½-inch) picture-frame or framing nails
- Hammer
- Instant adhesive (optional)
- 1 (6-foot) piece of jute

STEPS

1 Take the plant out of the pot. Brush off any loose soil but keep the root ball intact.

2 Lay out the wood slab in front of you on a table with the front side down. Affix the D-hooks and picture wire for hanging. (If you are using a wood slab as a mount, 1 D-hook might be sufficient and the picture wire unnecessary.) Turn the slab over so that it's face up.

3 On the slab, place a layer of moss between ¼ and ½ inch thick and the same diameter as the root ball of the fern.

4 Take your nails and hammer them halfway into the slab every inch around the moss, so that half of each nail is sticking out and half is in your slab. If the nails are having trouble staying in, dip them in superglue before hammering them in, and that should help them stay.

5 Put the plant on top of the moss bed with the halo of nails. Place it so that when hanging, the shield of the fern will be on top with the fronds falling toward the floor. Pack more moss around the root ball, making a blanket across it. Stay within the nails as much as possible.

6 Tie one end of the twine to one of the nails. Weave the twine around the nails, crossing the root ball and tightening as you go, working under the leaves, until you have firmly mounted the plant. When you can hold the slab vertically and the plant doesn't move, you have anchored it firmly. Tie the twine off and cut off the free end.

7 Run the plant gently under tepid water until the moss is saturated.

CARE: Mist your fern twice weekly or take it down and run it under tepid water until saturated once a week, allowing it to dry before rehanging. Like air plants, staghorn ferns prefer foliar fertilizer for feeding (see Plants with Special Needs, page 31).

THE KITCHEN GARDEN

While backyard gardens allow gardeners to show off their heirloom vegetables and fruiting trees and shrubs, what about folks who don't have a yard? Or, if you don't live in a warm place, how do you access the lively flavor and freshness of herbs and other tasty plants in the dead of winter? Easy—you plant food indoors.

In truth, there are many varieties of edibles, from thyme to garlic to ginger, that are successful indoors. Many of them make lovely houseplants on their own and reward with lovely and sometimes fragrant flowers or leaves that you can be certain is completely organic.

Veggie Reincarnation

Rather than composting your vegetable scraps or throwing them away, this project allows you to create beautiful new growth that becomes your next crop of veggies! Wait and harvest or simply enjoy their foliage and flowers.

While we've almost all done the avocado-pit-and-toothpicks-in-water trick once in our lives, only certain plants can be successfully reincarnated this way. Vegetables like celery or lettuce root easily in water, creating new shoots in a matter of days. Other odds and ends you can start directly in soil, where you'll soon see shoots that will turn into gorgeous plants. Below are the most successful and fun options for giving new life to your vegetable basket.

BASIL

Keep your bunch of fresh basil pert and ready for use by placing it in a glass or pitcher with fresh water, just like a bouquet. Change out the water every day or so, and you'll soon see the basil stems begin to send out roots.

MATERIALS

- 1 bunch basil
- 1 clear glass or jar

STEPS

1 Trim off the last ¼ inch of the basil stems and discard.

2 Fill the glass or jar with cool water and add basil. Place in bright light.

CARE: Change out the water every week. After about a week, you should begin to see roots emerge from the basil stems. Pot the basil in all-purpose potting soil once the roots have grown an inch or two. This could take anywhere from several weeks to months. Placed in a sunny windowsill and kept moist, the basil should continue to produce. Pinch off any flowers as they appear so that the basil does not go to seed.

CARROTS

The next time you're chopping up organic carrots for salad, retain the tops of the stem ends and nurture a beautiful plant. While indoor gardening isn't ideal for propagating carrots for eating—they need lots of room to grow and reach down into the soil—the resulting plants do put out lacy foliage and pretty white flowers. Once they go to seed, dry and save the seed to plant in your vegetable garden outside. This is fun to do when buying special varieties like purple or rainbow carrots.

MATERIALS

- 1 bunch organic carrots
- 1 shallow clear bowl or jar (such as an 8-ounce wide-mouth canning jar)

STEPS

1 If the carrots still have the greens attached, cut them off with a sharp knife about ½ inch above the top. Cut off the rest of the carrot, leaving a ½-inch chunk, including the top.

2 Place the carrot chunk in the bottom of the bowl or jar and add water so that just the very top of the carrot is exposed. Keep in bright light.

CARE: Change out the water every week. You should soon notice shoots growing out of the carrot top. Keep it in the water, or transplant the carrot to a pot with all-purpose potting soil, putting the bottom of the shoots at soil level. If keeping the carrot in water, you may want to transfer to a larger vessel and add a circulator to avoid stagnation. It takes a few months for carrots to grow and flower before going to seed.

GARLIC

Perhaps the easiest of them all, garlic gives you twice the reward, offering garlic shoots that are delicious on their own and offer a milder flavor similar to chives or green onions. As the garlic grows indoors, you can keep harvesting the shoots without harming the plant. In fact, harvesting the greens encourages the plant to put more energy into creating a larger head of garlic below the soil.

MATERIALS

- 1 (12-inch or larger) pot with drainage holes
- Organic all-purpose potting soil
- Organic garlic cloves
- Bacterial inoculant

STEPS

1 Fill the pot with a drainage layer followed by the potting soil.

2 Take two unpeeled garlic cloves and push them an inch or so below the surface on opposite sides of the pot, with the pointy ends up.

3 Water thoroughly with water to which bacterial inoculant has been added and place in bright light.

CARE: Water twice weekly or enough to keep the soil moist but not damp, and give it bright light. You'll soon see green shoots emerging from the soil. Use the shoots by keeping them cut to about 4 inches above the soil. This allows you to enjoy the greens and forces energy into the bulb. After about 9 months, you will know your garlic is ready to harvest once 4 to 8 of the outer shoots have shriveled and turned yellow.

GINGER OR TURMERIC

These tropical plants are difficult to grow outdoors in many climates but work well as indoor plants. They offer gorgeous foliage and flowers, as well as provide you with a fresh root to use grated or minced in your soups, stews, and curries. Organic gingerroot is available in most grocery stores. Fresh turmeric root, smaller in diameter with more wrinkled skin, is available in some higher-end markets as well as Asian groceries.

MATERIALS

- 1 (6-inch) pot with drainage holes
- Stones or pottery shards
- Organic all-purpose potting soil
- Organic gingerroot or turmeric root
- Bacterial inoculant

STEPS

1 Take the pot and add a drainage layer of stones.

2 Fill with potting soil.

3 Cut off a chunk of ginger or turmeric that contains a small round knob. That knob is a node, the site from which plants create new growth.

4 Plant the chunk with the knob facing up (cut side down) about an inch below the soil.

5 Water thoroughly with water to which bacterial inoculant has been added and place in bright light.

CARE: Water enough to keep the soil moist but not damp, and give it bright light. You'll soon see green shoots emerging from the soil where the node is planted. Once the root has at least doubled in size, which could take up to a year, you are ready to harvest. Poke your finger into the pot to tell when the ginger or turmeric is ready.

MORE GREAT OPTIONS TO BRING NEW LIFE TO YOUR VEGGIES

Celery

Begin with a whole head of celery. Cut off the stalks of the celery, leaving about an inch or two of the bottom of the head. Follow the instructions for carrots (page 141), placing the celery root side down in the water. When the emerging shoots reach 2 to 3 inches in length and the celery begins to send out roots, pot the celery in organic all-purpose potting soil and keep in moderate light.

Green Onions

Trim a bunch of green onions above the white part, leaving about ½ inch of green. Place the root ends down in fresh water just to cover (leaving any rubber bands around the bunch makes the rooting process much easier) and place in bright light. Pot the green onions in organic all-purpose potting soil when the shoots are an inch or two long. Use the green onion tops by snipping off as much as you need.

Lettuce

Don't throw out those lettuce cores! Harvest the leaves of the lettuce, leaving about an inch of plant attached to the root end. Follow the instructions for carrots (page 141), placing it root side down in the water. When the lettuce has new leaves about 2 inches in length and has established roots in the water, pot in organic all-purpose potting soil. You may harvest leaves from the outside of the head whenever you want to or, once the head has reached your desired size, cut off the whole head at soil level or pull up at the roots.

Other picks:
- Tender herbs
- Onions (any type)
- Lemongrass
- Greens, including spinach and kale

Living Herb Frame

Yes, this is an ambitious project. It requires both tools and patience. But if you're somewhat handy (or know someone who is), the result is a living frame that adorns your wall, ready and waiting for use in your next cooking adventure. (It would also make a pretty amazing gift.)

While there are a wide variety of herbs that can be grown inside, those with woodier stems and a trailing growth pattern will be most successful. There are many excellent choices just in the mint family (Lamiaceae), including thyme, oregano, and mint, among others. Try unusual specimens you can't find in the grocery store, such as lemon thyme or chocolate or pineapple mint. Make sure you use plastic mesh, as wire mesh will rust. Rolls are sold in garden stores and individual sheets can be found in craft stores or online. You can seal your own box; just ensure you use food-safe materials. Tall Earth makes excellent eco-safe products for this, or buy a ready-made box in a craft store or online.

MATERIALS

- Watertight wood box with an 8-by-10 or 5-by-7 inch opening
- Wood picture frame with the same inner dimensions as the box opening (8 by 10 or 5 by 7 inches)
- 1 roll or sheet ½-inch plastic mesh
- Mirror-hanging kit
- Organic all-purpose potting soil
- 4 L-brackets with wood screws
- Herb seeds or 12 small starts in 2-inch pots or cuttings of hardy, fast-growing herbs

SPECIALIZED TOOLS

- Staple gun
- Drill with ¼-inch bit

STEPS

1 Turn the frame over on a worktable so that the finished side is facing down. Cut a piece of mesh a bit larger than the opening. Staple it in place. Trim any excess and set aside. Determine which side of the box will be the top of the project once it is hanging on the wall. Using a ¼-inch bit, drill a small drainage hole in the opposite side of the box. Turn the box so that the bottom is facing you and affix hanging hardware from the mirror-hanging kit near what you'll want to be the top finished edge of your project.

2 Flip the box over and fill it with potting soil, mounding it in the center and slightly overfilling it so that the soil will be flush with the mesh once the frame is in place.

3 Place the frame over the box, wiggling it to ensure the soil spreads evenly.

4 Using the L-brackets and screws, secure the frame to the box so that it covers the box opening and forms a "lid" over the soil.

5 Use a chopstick to poke holes in the soil, and sprinkle in seeds or insert the stems of cuttings. If using seeds, sow fairly thickly. If using starts, remove from pots and brush away attached soil. Arrange the plants any way you like; take care to place trailing plants nearer the bottom edge away from the hanging hardware. If you need to stabilize the plants, you can use toothpicks pushed into the soil to help the herbs stay in place until they fully root. At this point, don't worry if there is soil on top of the mesh. Once the plants grow and begin to take, the root systems will keep the soil in place.

6 Water well with bacterial inoculant and allow it to drain. Set the frame flat in a sunny spot for 2 to 4 weeks if using cuttings or plant starts or 2 to 3 months for seeds, or until the plants are well established, before hanging. The longer you can allow it to sit before hanging, the more stable the project will be. Attach the hanging hardware and anchors to the wall, and hang your project.

CARE: When considering where you want to situate your herb frame, find a spot where the sun will shine head-on to the frame, preferably from a south- or west-facing window. This helps the plants grow straight rather than sideways seeking sun. The more sunlight you can give the herb frame, the faster the herbs will grow. To water the herbs, remove the frame from the wall and run them under a very gentle stream from the faucet. Allow the box to drain on the side with the hole to remove excess moisture before rehanging. Conversely, you can mist heavily with a spray bottle every few days. A potted plant placed under the drainage hole does a great job of catching drips!

BEST PICKS:

Lemon balm	Mint
Oregano	Sage
Thyme	

IV. PLANT STYLE

Now that you've mastered basic care techniques and gotten ideas for how you might use indoor plants, it's your turn to get creative. Because whether your home is midcentury modern or farmhouse eclectic, whether you live in the verdant Pacific Northwest or sunny, hot Southern California, whether you're looking to bring plants into your home, office, or both, there's a look for you. Here, I've curated some examples of favorite styles spanning a range of rooms and spaces. Use these images to get inspired and create your own look, being creative and bringing to them your own unique style.

Desert Boho   159

Eclectic   163

Midcentury   167

Minimal   171

Rustic   175

Urban Oasis   179

DESERT BOHO

You don't have to live in the Southwest to find inspiration in the region's earthy tones and sun-drenched beauty. Featuring a muted palette and natural materials like bone and hide, desert chic often highlights the structural drama of plants that call the desert home, such as succulents and cacti.

⟨ At this desert guesthouse, a majestic cowboy cactus holds sway, with both its height and color signaling its place at the top of the design hierarchy. The rest of the room evokes the severe beauty of a desert landscape, with animal hides, aged wood, metal, and hues of sun-bleached bone framing both window and bed. Showcase your statement succulent or cactus by keeping the supporting tones, including the pot, neutral.

∨ While many hanging plants are lush and leafy, here natural rope woven into a simple macramé hanger cradles the fierce spears of a potted cactus. To incorporate hanging succulents and cacti in your decor, use unglazed terra-cotta pots to echo the traditional sunbaked tiles of the Southwest.

Courtesy Ellie Lillstrom Photography

Courtesy Rich and Sara Combs of the Joshua Tree House

< The artful geometrics of kilim textiles on floor, daybed, and wall are complemented by the sculptural forms of desert cacti. Note that while both fabrics and plants provide texture, the relative uniformity of the succulents and their pots allows the patterns and sunset tones of the textiles to shine.

^ The upright growth habit of this showpiece cactus offers striking juxtaposition to the round mirror, light, and hats in this airy entryway. Get this look by layering natural elements, such as glazed tiles, terracotta, and wood, and playing with form and shape.

ECLECTIC

Some of the coziest spaces borrow looks from several decades, playing pieces of different textures, shapes, and colors off one another. It's no different for plants, with the eclectic style marked by a range of specimens of varying hues and growth habits and pots that add a design pop of their own.

˅ An oversized rubber tree makes a big statement when juxtaposed against pillows of varying textures, and furniture and flooring of textured wood grain. You don't always need multiple plants for an eclectic look. Let a large, bold plant take center stage on a background of layered fabrics, natural elements, and art pieces.

˅ A riot of succulent catcus paddles, jazzy striped calathea leaves, and a trailing variegated pothos is elevated by pots of varying hues and textures, drawing the eye. Rather than grouping like plants, dare to combine specimens with wildly diffferent textures, hues, and shapes.

Courtesy @ Desert Rose Succulents

⟨ A mix of plant types and containers create an enticing green corner. A vintage bar cart plays host to varied plant forms on two levels beneath a showpiece painting. Choose a bare space in your own home and then incorporate plants with many textures in containers of varied shapes and sizes. Rethink the table trope and reuse existing furniture pieces to showcase the plants. Incorporate paintings or sculpture to pull the look together.

⌄ There's nothing matchy-matchy about this look—with no container or plant the same size, shape, or color. Recreate this style by shopping garage sales or thrift stores to find unique containers that strike your fancy, and then integrate your plants into an artful tableau. Use shells, rocks, or other elements to add personality.

MIDCENTURY

Hitting pitch-perfect design notes borrowed from the '60s, midcentury is back, blending natural elements with iconic form. Simple planters and curved wood furniture set off plants with eye-catching structure, such as the fans of palm or bamboo, the sturdy tongues of snake plant, or the perforated leaves of monstera.

Courtesy Sarah Dorweiler

∧ The clean lines of the wood plant stand and simple white ceramic pot give way to leafy fronds arching against a white wall. A touch of natural elements, such as the woven basket, and use of graceful midcentury form makes this home office sing.

< The striking patterned leaves of monstera, or the Swiss cheese plant, offer an outsized design element to this living room. The overlapping squares of the curio shelf and the bright colors of the geometric throw pillow help anchor this plant's big personality. Balance the bluster of loud plants with dusty tones and clean lines in the surrounding pieces.

< Warm up a cool midcentury vibe by playing with an abundance of greenery. The richly patterned and textured leaves of potted dieffenbachia echo throw pillows and an Oriental rug. Plants also surprise with unexpected placement—swinging above the couch—and shapes atop the armoire.

∨ Bold leaf shapes lend themselves beautifully to a midcentury aesthetic. Featured here are the sturdy pillars of snake plant, a conical cactus, and large-leafed philodendron, all set off by the crisp white of the lamp and a luxurious rocker.

MINIMAL

The minimal, monochrome look of '80s modern interior design has come roaring back, marked by clean, crisp lines and a white-on-white palette. Minimal interiors are a blank canvas offering the perfect backdrop for indoor plants, allowing them to star and serve as focal points for the room.

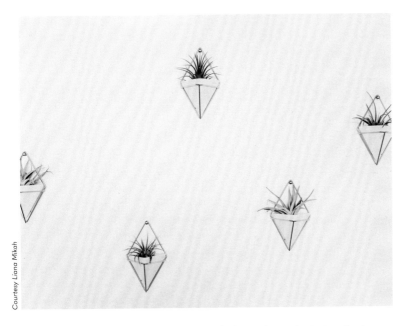

Courtesy Liana Mikah

‹ You needn't group plants to make them the focal point. Minimalism celebrates the loneliest number—a solitary specimen in a neutral container strikes a perfect pose against a black-and-white background. Here, an entryway gets pop from a potted fan palm. Instead of clustering, choose a single plant with a striking shape or color and let it take a place of honor.

^ As an alternative to hanging brass himmeli (page 121), the geometric structures are mounted as sconces on a white wall. Air plants of slightly different tones and shapes are showcased perfectly in this setting. The use of three sconces illustrates an interior design tenet—odd numbers always read best. Arrange three, five, or more sconces against a white wall, and voila!

Courtesy Sophie Davies, A Considered Life

⟨ A hanging kokedama palm lends whimsy to a bedroom that is otherwise minimal in style and color. Plants—whether because of their shape, size, or placement—can bring an element of surprise to an otherwise neutral palette. Provide pop to your own minimalist design by hanging a plant in an unexpected location or using unique containers. Kokedama are commonly seen in bathrooms and kitchens but are charming additions to any room.

⌃ Green plants provide a corner of cool tranquility in this classic white bathroom. Here, a golden pothos hangs above the bathtub, providing elevation and drawing the eye, while the lacy foliage of an asparagus fern is reflected by a well-placed mirror. Bathrooms often lend themselves to a minimal design aesthetic and provide the humidity many tropical plants and ferns love. Be aware of how much light your bathroom gets—choose a plant such as pothos or the cast-iron plant for darker, humid locations.

RUSTIC

The folksy warmth of rustic style leverages distressed metals and containers along with natural wood to create rooms that feel well loved and bring the outdoors in. Houseplants fit beautifully into a rustic aesthetic, nestled in galvanized tins or copper pots or mounted in natural fabrics.

Courtesy Jaime-Anne Etherington (Rustic Yogi)

⟨ A long shelf fashioned of reclaimed wood creates a rustic perch for the plants lining this entryway. To capture this look, place pots on rough-hewn shelves, tables, or a vintage wooden ladder.

⌃ In this cozy living room, tongues of variegated snake plant play off the softer textures of a macramé wall hanging and a crocheted throw, while a repurposed yellow crock makes a statement pot. For a rustic vibe, look for vintage milk jugs or cooking vessels to home your plants.

Courtesy Pistils Nursery, Portland, Oregon

⟨ This antique rolling cart hosts an army of cacti and haworthia in uniform terra-cotta pots, joined by feathers that ape stems and leaves sprouting from a vintage jar. The white-washed exposed brick and cactus housed in a snakeskin-look basket add rustic texture and interest.

∧ Once you've mastered the art of mounting staghorn ferns (page 133), create a showpiece wall by grouping them en masse. Affixed to wood slabs and nestled in vintage burlap, this charming herd of staghorns adds both rich color and texture in a vertical space.

URBAN OASIS

Vines tumble off shelves, leaves enliven windowsills, and even the floor "sprouts" potted specimens. Create your own urban oasis by going overboard with your groupings, mixing plants of different growth habits and colors and inundating one wall, shelf, or nook.

‹ A riot of color and texture creates a living wall, carving this sitting area out from a larger loft space. Consider every surface, from floor to wall to ceiling, a potential home for plants of all sizes and growth habits and incorporate different hues, textures, and variegated leaves to pull it all together.

⌄ A climbing vine creates a frame for lush leaves, both in plant and print form. Pair botanical drawings with living "art" to form a verdant gallery.

Courtesy Brina Blum

‹ A cozy attic bedroom feels anything but small thanks to a lofty cascading vine and a headboard crafted of wooden pallets and potted plants. When creating your own urban oasis, don't forget about bathrooms and bedrooms where lush greenery works to wholly transform the space.

^ The cheery simplicity of this breakfast nook is enlivened by a panoply of plants that climb, creep, drape, and mound from the shelf and floor. The pop of vibrant orange that peeks through the tangle of lush foliage offers balance and focal interest.

ACKNOWLEDGMENTS

I'd like to thank my friends, family, and staff for helping me learn and my business grow. Also, thanks to the lovely people at Girl Friday Productions, Sasquatch, and photographer Sara Mark for bringing my vision to life.

   I would also like to thank all the wonderful photographers, stylists, and plant lovers who contributed their work to this book, including Jessica White, Hannah Leonard, Rich and Sara Combs, Ellie Lillstrom, Plant Shop Seattle, Desert Rose Succulents, Emily Katz, Mandy Bollegraf, Scott Cain, Christine Kelso, Sophie Davies, Byron Beach Abodes, Jaime-Anne Etherington, Jamie Song, and Kimberly Wynn. Also, thanks to Pistils Nursery, a specialty plant shop and mercantile in Portland, Oregon. Their mounted staghorn ferns and other botanically inspired living works of art help people seeking simple, beautiful ways to bring a bit of the outside in. Finally, thanks to Natasha Sidhu (@la_sidhu), a London-based, jungle-loving plant addict with an immense love for botanically bohemian interiors and all things green.

RESOURCES

BENEFITS OF INDOOR PLANTS

A 1989 NASA study provides the best research we have on the benefits of indoor plants.

NASA INDOOR LANDSCAPE PLANT STUDY: ntrs.nasa.gov/archive /nasa/casi.ntrs.nasa.gov/19930073077.pdf

PLANT TOXICITY INFORMATION

If you have animals or small children and are concerned about plant toxicity, you can start with the National Capital Poison Center and the Plant Toxicity Database for information. However, plant databases aren't always up to date or comprehensive, so you may also want to bring a sample of plants you're concerned about to your vet or pediatrician to discuss any potential toxicity.

NATIONAL CAPITAL POISON CENTER: www.poison.org/articles/plant

PLANT TOXICITY DATABASE: www.aspca.org/pet-care/animal -poison-control/toxic-and-non-toxic-plants

In the event that a pet or child ingests a plant, call:

ANIMAL POISON CONTROL: 1-888-426-4435 (a $65 consulting fee may apply)

POISON CONTROL HOTLINE: 1-800-222-1222 (there is no charge for consulting Poison Control)

WHERE TO SHOP

I recommend buying plants and other supplies in person at a local plant supplier that you love. Small stores like Urban Sprouts in Renton, Washington, can always use your support—and they're going to provide you with customer service and education that you just won't get at a big-box nursery or garden store.

If you happen to live in a state where marijuana is legal, you can often buy indoor growing supplies at cannabis stores. If you live in an area without a local indoor nursery, you can also purchase plants and supplies online. For general online indoor plant shopping, you can try my store, Urban Sprouts (Urban-Sprouts.com/shop), or The Sill (TheSill.com).

I've included a few of my favorite products and their sources below.

AQUATIC SUBSTRATE: My favorite substrate for aquatic plants is Gro Pro (AquariumPlants.com).

COMPOST: At Urban Sprouts we use Cedar Grove brand (Cedar-Grove.com) because it's local to Seattle. It's best to use whatever is local and organic in your area. To find a good compost brand in your region, use this searchable database of regional composters by the Composting Council (CompostingCouncil.org/compostmap/).

FERTILIZER: I love this bacterial inoculant, which comes in a small pouch that makes 3 gallons of liquid fertilizer. It's available at the Urban Sprouts online store (Urban-Sprouts.com/product-page/bacterial-innoculant-fertilizer). For aquatic plants, I use Aquafertz pellets (AquariumPlants.com).

HIMMELI TUBES: You can buy precut himmeli tubes online at Etsy (Etsy.com). One store I like in particular is Yakutum (Yakutum.com).

LIGHTING: If you lack good natural lighting, Agrobrite brand grow lights are less than $20 and don't cast a strange color light—meaning you can use these as general lighting in spaces that lack natural lighting, for example, a bathroom. While you can't buy Agrobrite lights directly, HydroFarm provides a resource for local retailers (HydroFarm.com).

MOSS: For moss, I recommend SuperMoss sphagnum moss sheets (SuperMoss.com).

POTTING SOIL: Black Gold is a readily available brand that is consistently good and authentically organic (BlackGold.bz).

SEALANTS: For an eco-safe sealant, I recommend the Tall Earth brand (TallEarth.com).

WATERING: Blumat, an Austrian company, makes excellent terra-cotta water-siphon spikes (Blumats.com).

INDEX

Note: Page numbers in *italic* refer to photographs.

A

Acanthaceae (nerve plant), *66*, 67
air filtering, best plants for, x
air plant (Bromeliaceae)
    about, *38*, 39
    cuttings from, 23
    fertilizer for, 31
    hanging globe project, *92*, 93–94,
      95
    minimalist style and, 171, *171*
    reflected pyramid himmeli project,
      120, 121–127
algae buildup, 97, 100
aquatic plants, 37
    fertilizer for, 31, 186
    types, 71–73
    See also water gardens
Araceae (dieffenbachia), 60, *61*
Araceae (peace lily), 50, *51*
Araceae (pothos), 68, *69*
Arecaceae (palm), 44, *45*
Asparagaceae (cast-iron plant), 56, *57*
Asparagaceae (dracaena), *62*, 63
Asparagaceae (lucky bamboo), *70*, 71
Asparagaceae (snake plant), 46, *47*

B

bacterial inoculant, 30, 186
basil, 139
Beaucarnea recurvata (ponytail
    palm), 44, *44*
beginners, plants for, 53, *53*
bell jars, 81
biochar, 81
Blumat, 18, *18*, 187
bowl gardens. *See* terrariums and
    bowl gardens
Bromeliaceae. *See* air plant

C

cachepots, 16
cactus (Cactaceae), 15, 21
    about, 40, *41*
    bowl project for, 91, *91*
    potting soil for, 11
calathea (Marantaceae), 54, 55
carrots, *140*, 141
cast-iron plant (Asparagaceae), 56, *57*
celery, 146, *147*
citrus (Rutaceae), 31, *58*, 59

Cladophoraceae. *See* marimo
climbing plants. *See* hanging and
    vertical gardens
cloches, 81
compost-tea granules, 30
Crassula ovata (jade plant), 53, *53*
Crassulaceae (echeveria), *42*, 43
Crassulaceae (sempervivum), *52*, 53
cuttings, 23

D

desert boho style, *158*, 159–161, *160*
desert plants, 37
    cactus bowl project, 91, *91*
    hanging air plant globe project, *92*,
      93–94, *95*
    potting soil for, 11
    reflected pyramid himmeli project,
      120, 121–127, 171, *171*
    types, 39–47
    watering guidelines, *14*
devil's ivy. *See* pothos
dieffenbachia (Araceae), 60, *61*
dracaena (Asparagaceae), *62*, 63
drainage layer, 10
drought-tolerant plants, 90
duck lettuce. *See* floating stems
    project
dumb cane plant. *See* dieffenbachia
dwarfing, 27

E

echeveria (Crassulaceae), *42*, 43
eclectic style, *162*, 163–164, *165*
environmental zones, 36–37

F

feeding, 29–31, 186
fern (Polypodiaceae), *48*, 49
fertilizing. *See* feeding
ficus (Moraceae), 64, *65*
fish, in water gardens, 107
floating stems project, *108*, 109–110,
    111
foliar fertilizer, 31

G

garlic, 143
ginger, 144, *145*
green onions, 146

H

hanging and vertical gardens, *112*, 113
  hanging air plant globe, *92*, 93–94, *95*
  kokedama, *114*, 115–118, *117*, *119*, *172*, 173
  living herb frame, *148*, 149–152, *151*
  mounted staghorn fern, *132*, 133–134, *135*, 177, *177*
  reflected pyramid himmeli, *120*, 121–127, 171, *171*
  vertical vines, *128*, 129–130, *131*
  watering tips, 18
Haworthia fasciata (zebra cactus), 40, *40*
hen and chicks. *See* sempervivum
herb frame, *148*, 149–152, *151*
himmeli plant holders, *120*, 121–127, 171, *171*

J

jade plant (*Crassula ovata*), 53, *53*

K

kitchen garden, *136*, 137
  living herb frame project, *148*, 149–152, *151*
  veggie reincarnation project, *138*, 139–146
kokedama
  best plants for, 118
  minimalist style and, *172*, 173
  project for, *114*, 115–118, *117*, *119*
  string choices for, 118

L

landscape, underwater, *102*, 103–106, *105*
lettuce, 146
lighting conditions, 19
lighting equipment, 187
lucky bamboo (Asparagaceae), *70*, 71

M

Maranta leuconeura (prayer plant), 55, *55*
Marantaceae (calathea), *54*, 55
marimo (Cladophoraceae)
  about, *72*, *73*
  habitat project, *98*, 99–100, *101*
midcentury style, *166*, 167–169, *168*
minimalist style, *170*, 171–173, *172*
Moraceae (ficus), *64*, 65

moss, 49
moss balls. *See* marimo
mother-in-law's tongue. *See* snake plant
mounted staghorn fern, 49, *132*, 133–134, *135*, 177, *177*

N

nerve plant (Acanthaceae), *66*, 67
nutrients. *See* feeding

O

onions, green, 146
overwatering, 16, 17

P

palm (Arecaceae), 44, *45*
peace lily (Araceae), 50, *51*
peacock plant. *See* calathea
plant toxicity information, 185
planting kit, *4*, 5–7
plants, benefits of indoor, ix–x, 185
plants, safety of, 7
plants and supplies, resources for, 186–187
Polypodiaceae (fern), *48*, 49
ponytail palm (*Beaucarnea recurvata*), 44, *44*
pothos (Araceae), 68, *69*
pots, choosing, 9
potting plants, *8*, 9–12
  drainage layer for, 10
  loosening roots, 10
  pots, choosing, 9
  root-bound, trimming, 27
  soils, by plant type, 11
  steps for, 12, *13*
  transplant shock, 11
  when to repot, 9, 12, 17
prayer plant (*Maranta leuconeura*), 55, *55*
pruning, 21
  branches, 21–23
  roots, 24–27, *26*

R

rattlesnake plant. *See* calathea
reflected pyramid himmeli, *120*, 121–127, 171, *171*
repotting. *See* potting plants
resources, 185–187
root-bound plants, 17, 27
roots, loosening up, 10

roots, pruning, 24–27, *26*
rustic style, *174*, 175–177, *176*
Rutaceae (citrus), 31, *58*, 59

S

safety for children and pets, 7
sealants, 187
sempervivum (Crassulaceae), *52*, 53
snake plant (Asparagaceae), *46*, 47
soil, healthy, 30
soils, by plant type, 11
soils, resources for, 186, 187
Spathiphyllum. See peace lily
spider plant (*Chlorophytum comosum*), 27
staghorn fern. *See* mounted staghorn fern
succulents
    best types for beginners, 53, *53*
    bowl project for, *86*, 87–90, *89*
    cuttings from, 23
    drought-tolerant and low-water varieties, 90
    See also desert plants; sempervivum

T

temperate plants, 37
    potting soil for, 11
    types, 49–53
    watering guidelines, *14*
terrariums and bowl gardens, *78*, 79
    cactus bowl project, 91, *91*
    drought-tolerant and low-water plants for, 90
    hanging air plant globe project, *92*, 93–94, *95*
    moss in, 49
    root trimming and, 27
    succulent bowl project, *86*, 87–90, *89*
    tropical terrarium project, *80*, 81–84, *83*
    tropical terrarium project; custom variation, 85
    watering tips, 17
Thirsty Light, 18
tillandsia. *See* air plant
tools, *4*, 5–7
trailing plants. *See* hanging and vertical gardens
transplant shock, 11
tropical plants, 37
    potting soil for, 11

terrarium project for, *80*, 81–84, *83*
terrarium project for; custom variation, 85
types, 55–69
watering guidelines, *14*
turmeric, 144

U

underwater landscape, *102*, 103–106, *105*
underwatering, 17
urban oasis style, *178*, 179–181, *180*

V

veggie reincarnation project, *138*, 139–146
vines/vertical gardens. *See* hanging and vertical gardens

W

water gardens, *96*, 97
    algae buildup in, 97, 100
    best plants for, 106
    fertilizer for, 31
    fish in, 107
    floating stems project, *108*, 109–110, *111*
    marimo habitat project, *98*, 99–100, *101*
    root trimming, 27
    underwater landscape project, *102*, 103–106, *105*
    See also aquatic plants
watering, 15–18
    drought-tolerant and low-water plants, 90
    general guidelines, *14*, 15–16
    hanging plants, 18
    overwatering/underwatering, signs of, 17
    schedule for, 16
    technology and self-watering systems, 18, *18*
    terrariums and closed containers, 17
    watering cans and misters, 5–6, *6*, 84

Z

zebra cactus (*Haworthia fasciata*), 40, *40*
ZZ plant (*Zamioculcas zamiifolia*), 56, *56*

PHOTO CREDITS

Cover
© Rich Stapleton

Unless otherwise noted, interior photography was provided by © Sara Mark Photography.

Front Matter
pp. ii–iii: © Belle Hunt/Unsplash.com. pp. iv–v: © Chris Lee/Unsplash.com. p. viii: © Mike Marquez/Unsplash.com.

Part I: Plant Basics
p. xii: © Bart Zimny/Unsplash.com. p. 3: © Kara Michelle/Unsplash.com.

Part II: Plant Guide
p. 32: © John Salzarulo/Unsplash.com. p. 35: © Mike Marquez/Unsplash.com. p. 36: © Annie Spratt/Unsplash.com. p. 40: © Alvin Engler/Unsplash.com. p. 53: © Duskbabe/Dreamstime.com. p. 55: © Lost Mountain Studio/Shutterstock.com. p. 56: © Sharaf Maksumov/Dreamstime.com. p. 58: © Shutterstock/tkyoy.

Part III: Plant Projects
p. 107: © AnnaDona/Shutterstock.com. p. 112: © La Florida studio/commons.wikimedia.org. p. 128: Jamie Song @jamies_jungle.

Part IV: Plant Style
p. 154: Jamie Song @jamies_jungle. p. 157: © Chua Bing Quan/Unsplash.com.

DESERT BOHO p. 158, 161: Rich and Sara Combs of the Joshua Tree House. p. 159: Ellie Lillstrom Photography. p. 160: Jessica White Photography, styling by Hannah Leonard of Loom and Kiln.

ECLECTIC p. 162: © Emily Katz, modernmacrame.com. p. 163: © Desert Rose Succulents. pp. 164–165: Plant Shop Seattle.

MIDCENTURY p. 166: Scott Cain @tropicaloco. p. 167: Sarah Dorweiler. p. 168: Mandy Bollegraf @mandybollegraf. p. 169: Christine Kelso @ workhardplanthard.

MINIMAL p. 170: Alexandra Gorn. p. 171: Liana Mikah. p. 172: Jessie Prince © Byron Beach Abodes. p. 173: Sophie Davies, *A Considered Life*.

RUSTIC p. 174: © SoNelly/Shutterstock.com. p. 175: Jaime-Anne Etherington (Rustic Yogi). p. 176: Natasha Sidhu @la_sidhu. p. 177: Pistils Nursery; Portland, Oregon.

URBAN OASIS p. 178: Jamie Song @jamies_jungle. p. 179: Prudence Earl. p. 180: Kim Wynn @kim.wynn. p. 181: Brina Blum.

Back Matter
p. 184: © Milada Vigerova/Unsplash.com. p. 188: © Scott Webb/Unsplash.com. p. 196: © Elsa Noblet.

Back Cover
© Scott Webb/Unsplash.com

ABOUT THE AUTHOR

JEN STEARNS was born and raised in the historic Wallingford neighborhood of Seattle, where she spent time in her mother's vegetable garden as a child. A lifelong plant lover, she has a BS in environmental science from the University of Washington and has found her calling empowering beginning gardeners to create spaces brimming with personality and life. She is the owner of Urban Sprouts, a plant storefront, online store, and mobile unit that offers hands-on classes, private events, and subscription services to make plant care simple and enjoyable. She lives with her husband in Renton, Washington.